risotto

risotto

over 50 fresh and innovative recipes
for the creative cook

CHRISTINE INGRAM

LORENZ BOOKS

For all recipes, **quantities** are given in both **metric** and **imperial** measures and, where appropriate, measures are also given in **standard cups** and **spoons**. Follow one set but not a mixture because they are **not interchangeable**.

Standard **spoon** and **cup measures** are **level**.
1 tsp = 5ml, 1 tbsp = 15ml, 1 cup = 250ml/8 fl oz

Australian standard **tablespoons** are 20ml. Australian readers should use 3 tsp in place of 1 tbsp for measuring small quantities of gelatine, cornflour, salt etc.

Medium eggs are used unless otherwise stated.

The recipes in this book appear in **Rice & Risotto**.

First published in 2000 by Lorenz Books

Lorenz Books is an imprint of Anness Publishing Limited
Hermes House, 88–89 Blackfriars Road, London SE1 8HA

© Anness Publishing Limited 2000

A CIP catalogue record for this book is available from the British Library

Publisher Joanna Lorenz
Editor Felicity Forster
Design Wherefore Art?
Photography Dave King
Food for photography Jennie Shapter, Lucy McKelvie
Stylists Jo Harris, Helen Trent
Recipes Carla Capalbo, Kit Chan, Roz Denny, Rafi Fernandez, Silvana Franco, Deh-Ta Hsiung, Shezad Husain, Christine Ingram, Soheila Kimberley, Masaki Ko, Elizabeth Lambert Ortiz, Ruby Le Bois, Sallie Morris
Editorial reader Diane Ashmore
Production controller Joanna King

10 9 8 7 6 5 4 3 2 1

risotto

introduction

Making risotto is **more** than mere cooking – it's a SENSUOUS experience as you gradually add **liquid** to the grateful grain and **watch** it swell to tender **perfection**. Difficult? Not a bit of it. If you can **stir**, you can **star** as a risotto cook. This book provides the perfect **introduction** to the art and also invites you to try other **savoury** and sweet rice dishes from around the **world**.

varieties & techniques

RISOTTO IS THE **PERFECT** DISH FOR OUR TIMES – **NUTRITIOUS**, **DELICIOUS**, **SIMPLE** TO COOK AND **IDEAL** FOR **ENTERTAINING**.

It is true that it must be made at the last moment, but that is part of its charm. If you have everything ready before you start, the actual cooking is so straightforward that you can safely invite your guests to join you in the kitchen, or have them sit up at the table if your kitchen and dining room are one. That way you won't miss out on the pre-dinner conversation, and they'll get to feel part of the process, especially if you delegate simple tasks like opening wine, grating Parmesan or chopping parsley.

THE RIGHT RICE

The secret of a superb risotto lies in using the very best ingredients. The rice must be sufficiently starchy to cook to creamy perfection, but retain a firm "bite" at the centre of the grain. Since risotto was invented in Italy, it is not surprising that the best rice for the job comes from that country. Arborio is the most popular variety, and is suitable for all types of risotto, but it has a very large grain and can become slightly soggy if cooked for too long. This is why risotto is removed from the heat while it is still slightly firm, and allowed to rest (and finish cooking) before being served.

Carnaroli gives an even better result than Arborio. It holds its shape well after cooking, and the centre remains satisfyingly firm. Look out, too, for Vialone Nano, a plump grain with many of the characteristics of Carnaroli.

At one time, all these grains would simply have been labelled "risotto rice", but nowadays, thanks to the huge popularity of this delicious dish, you should be able to track down specific types quite easily, and may even encounter less common varieties such as Baldo or Roma.

TOP (CLOCKWISE FROM TOP LEFT): Arborio, Carnaroli and Vialone Nano.
LEFT (CLOCKWISE FROM TOP): Instant risottos flavoured with cuttlefish, tomatoes, saffron and spinach.

STOCK SECRETS

The next ingredient to consider is the stock. Since this is primarily what flavours the rice, it is essential to use a good one. Make your own stock, if possible, but if you don't have time, buy a good quality carton from the supermarket. Recipes state which stock to use, but if in doubt, use chicken or vegetable stock. What matters is depth – not strength – of flavour, so avoid using stock cubes.

The stock needs to be simmering when you add it to the rice. It is a good idea to have slightly more than the recipe recommends, since risotto cookery isn't an exact science. Factors such as the variety and age of the rice, the size of the pan, and how much liquid is released by other ingredients all affect the outcome, so be prepared to be flexible. You'll soon learn to recognize the precise moment when the rice is cooked to perfection.

OTHER INGREDIENTS

The ingredients that can be added to risotto are legion, and are limited only by the imagination of the cook and the gallantry of the guests. Before you raid the fridge, however, bear in mind that the best risottos are often the simplest. A splash of wine, a little cheese, a few fresh herbs - these are the ingredients that will enrich the dish, while still allowing the flavour of the rice and stock to shine through.

THE EQUIPMENT

You need no special equipment for making risotto. Purists advise using a large, heavy-bottomed pan with straight sides, but a deep frying pan can be used instead, and there's nothing wrong with a wok, provided that it has a lid or you have some other means of covering it while the rice rests. Other than that, all you need is a wooden spoon, and a ladle for adding the stock.

LEFT, FROM TOP TO BOTTOM: Fresh shavings of Parmesan may be used on their own or to complement other ingredients; delicate-flavoured herbs such as thyme, sage, coriander and tarragon can be stirred into the cooked rice; onions and garlic are essential ingredients in a good risotto; fresh green vegetables such as courgettes, spinach and asparagus add texture to dishes; chicken fillets and gammon should be browned before stirring into the rice; similarly, fish and shellfish such as salmon fillets, haddock, plaice and tiger prawns are generally cooked before being added about three-quarters of the way through cooking.

TOASTING THE RICE

This is the first stage in the process of making risotto. The fat (usually butter, but sometimes oil) is heated in the pan. Aromatics such as onion or garlic are added next, but these are merely sweated in the fat, never browned. The rice should be added all at once, and should be stirred constantly, until each grain is evenly coated in fat. Keep stirring until the rice grains are shiny and opaque. At this stage the rice will be very hot, and will welcome the first splash of liquid, whether this be wine or stock, responding gratefully with a sigh of steam: *il sospiro*.

A STIRRING STORY

From this moment on, the rice needs to be stirred constantly, but as the process never takes more than 20 minutes, and you will still have a hand free to raise a glass to your lips, the process isn't particularly arduous. As soon as the first batch of stock has been absorbed by the rice, add another ladleful, and when that disappears, add some more. Continue in this fashion, stirring soothingly all the while, until you have added most of the liquid, and about a quarter of an hour has passed.

TASTE TEST

You'll be able to tell when the rice is almost ready, because it will start to look creamy, and you will be able to see the furrow made by the spoon. Taste a grain. The rice should be *al dente* – virtually tender, but still a little hard at the centre. At this stage you may be advised to add cheese or extra butter, and should check the seasoning. Remove the pan from the heat, cover it and leave it to rest for about 5 minutes.

SERVING SUGGESTIONS

In Italy, risotto is served as a separate course, before the meat and vegetables. It makes a superb starter, and it is a good idea to follow it with a crisp salad of fresh leaves, as a contrast to its creaminess, and to cleanse the palate. Parmesan is often served with risotto, especially if it is also an integral ingredient, and can be shaved or grated. Always buy Parmesan in one piece and prepare it only when needed.

ABOVE: Risi e Bisi topped with fresh Parmesan shavings.

cheese

two cheese risotto

method

THIS UNDENIABLY **RICH** AND **CREAMY** RISOTTO IS JUST THE THING TO SERVE ON COLD **WINTER** EVENINGS WHEN EVERYONE NEEDS **WARMING** UP.

ingredients

7.5ml/1½ tsp **olive oil**

50g/2oz/4 tbsp **butter**

1 **onion**, finely chopped

1 **garlic** clove, crushed

275g/10oz/1½ cups **risotto rice**, preferably Vialone Nano

175ml/6fl oz/¾ cup **dry white wine**

1 litre/1¾ pints/4 cups simmering **vegetable** or **chicken stock**

75g/3oz/¾ cup **fontina cheese**, cubed

50g/2oz/⅔ cup freshly grated **Parmesan cheese**, plus extra to serve

salt and freshly ground **black pepper**

1 Heat the olive oil with half the butter in a pan and gently fry the onion and garlic for 5–6 minutes until soft. Add the rice and cook, stirring all the time, until the grains are coated in fat and have become slightly translucent around the edges.

2 Stir in the wine. Cook, stirring, until the liquid has been absorbed, then add a ladleful of hot stock. Stir until the stock has been absorbed, then add the remaining stock in the same way, waiting for each quantity of stock to be absorbed before adding more.

3 When the rice is half cooked, stir in the fontina cheese, and continue cooking and adding stock. Keep stirring the rice all the time.

4 When the risotto is creamy and the grains are tender but still have a bit of "bite", stir in the remaining butter and the Parmesan. Season, then remove the pan from the heat, cover and leave to rest for 3–4 minutes before serving.

quick risotto

method

THIS IS RATHER A **CHEAT'S** RISOTTO AS IT DEFIES ALL THE RULES THAT INSIST THE STOCK IS ADDED GRADUALLY. INSTEAD, THE RICE IS COOKED **QUICKLY** IN A CONVENTIONAL WAY, AND THE OTHER INGREDIENTS ARE SIMPLY THROWN IN AT THE **LAST MINUTE**. IT TASTES **GOOD** FOR ALL THAT.

ingredients

275g/10oz/1½ cups **risotto rice**

1 litre/1¾ pints/4 cups simmering **chicken stock**

115g/4oz/1 cup **mozzarella cheese**, cut into small cubes

2 **egg yolks**

30ml/2 tbsp freshly grated **Parmesan cheese**

75g/3oz cooked **ham**, cut into small cubes

30ml/2 tbsp chopped fresh **parsley**

salt and freshly ground **black pepper**

freshly grated **Parmesan cheese**, to serve

1 Put the rice in a pan. Pour in the stock, bring to the boil and then cover and simmer for about 18–20 minutes until the rice is tender.

2 Remove the pan from the heat and quickly stir in the mozzarella, egg yolks, Parmesan, ham and parsley. Season well with salt and pepper.

3 Cover the pan and stand for 2–3 minutes to allow the cheese to melt, then stir again. Pile into warmed serving bowls and serve immediately, with extra Parmesan cheese.

THIS **CLASSIC** RISOTTO IS ALWAYS SERVED WITH THE **HEARTY** BEEF STEW, OSSO BUCO, BUT ALSO MAKES A **DELICIOUS** FIRST COURSE OR **LIGHT** SUPPER DISH IN ITS OWN RIGHT.

ingredients

about 1.2 litres/2 pints/5 cups **beef** or **chicken stock**

good pinch of **saffron strands**

75g/3oz/6 tbsp **butter**

1 **onion**, finely chopped

275g/10oz/1½ cups **risotto rice**

75g/3oz/1 cup freshly grated **Parmesan cheese**

salt and freshly ground **black pepper**

risotto alla milanese

method

SERVES 4

1 Bring the stock to the boil, then reduce to a low simmer. Ladle a little stock into a small bowl. Add the saffron strands and leave to infuse.

2 Melt 50g/2oz/4 tbsp of the butter in a large saucepan until foaming. Add the onion and cook gently for about 3 minutes, stirring frequently, until softened but not browned.

3 Add the rice. Stir until the grains start to swell and burst, then add a few ladlefuls of the stock, with the saffron liquid and salt and pepper to taste. Stir over a low heat until the stock has been absorbed. Add the remaining stock, a few ladlefuls at a time, allowing the rice to absorb all the liquid before adding more, and stirring constantly. After 20–25 minutes, the rice should be just tender and the risotto golden yellow, moist and creamy.

4 Gently stir in about two-thirds of the grated Parmesan and the remaining butter. Heat through until the butter has melted, then taste for seasoning. Transfer the risotto to a warmed serving bowl or platter and serve hot, with the remaining grated Parmesan served separately.

risotto with parmesan

THIS **TRADITIONAL** RISOTTO IS SIMPLY FLAVOURED WITH **GRATED PARMESAN** CHEESE AND **GOLDEN**, FRIED CHOPPED ONION.

method

SERVES 3–4

1 Heat the stock in a saucepan, and leave to simmer until needed.

2 Melt two-thirds of the butter in a large heavy-based saucepan or deep frying pan. Stir in the onion, and cook gently until soft and golden.

3 Add the rice and stir to coat the grains with butter. After 1–2 minutes, pour in the white wine. Raise the heat slightly, and cook until the wine evaporates. Add one small ladleful of the hot stock. Cook until the stock has been absorbed, stirring constantly.

4 Gradually add the remaining stock, a little at a time, allowing the rice to absorb the liquid before adding more, and stirring constantly. After 20–30 minutes the rice should be creamy and *al dente*. Season to taste.

5 Remove the pan from the heat. Stir in the remaining butter and the Parmesan cheese. Taste again for seasoning. Allow the risotto to rest for 3–4 minutes before serving, garnished with basil leaves and shavings of Parmesan, if you like.

> ### cook's tip
> If you run out of stock when cooking the risotto, use hot water, but do not worry if the rice is done before you have used up all the stock.

ingredients

1 litre/1¾ pints/4 cups **beef**, **chicken** or **vegetable stock**
65g/2½oz/5 tbsp **butter**
1 small **onion**, finely chopped
275g/10oz/1½ cups **risotto rice**
120ml/4fl oz/½ cup **dry white wine**
75g/3oz/1 cup freshly grated **Parmesan cheese**, plus extra to garnish
basil leaves, to garnish
salt and freshly ground **black pepper**

THIS CLASSIC **CHEESE** RISOTTO CAN BE MADE MORE **SUBSTANTIAL** BY ADDING **CUBES** OF SMALL, PEELED AND SEEDED **BUTTERNUT SQUASH** WITH THE RICE.

ingredients

750ml/1¼ pints/3 cups **chicken**
  or **vegetable stock**
good pinch of **saffron strands**
  or 1 sachet **saffron powder**
90ml/6 tbsp **olive oil**
1 **onion**, finely chopped
275g/10oz/1½ cups **risotto**
  rice
400ml/14fl oz/1⅔ cups **dry**
  white wine
115g/4oz/1¼ cups freshly grated
  Parmesan cheese
freshly ground **black pepper**

parmesan & saffron risotto

method

SERVES 4

1 Bring the stock to the boil and reduce it to a low simmer. Ladle a little of it into a small bowl. Sprinkle the saffron strands or powder over the stock and leave to infuse.

2 Heat 60ml/4 tbsp of the oil in a large saucepan. Add the onion and cook gently for about 5 minutes, stirring frequently, until softened.

3 Add the rice and stir to coat the grains with oil. After 1–2 minutes, add the infused saffron mixture, with the wine and a small ladleful of the simmering stock. Cook until the liquid has been absorbed, stirring constantly.

4 Gradually add the remaining stock, a little at a time, allowing the rice to absorb the liquid before adding more, and stirring constantly. After 20–30 minutes the rice should be creamy and *al dente*.

5 When the rice is cooked, gently stir in about half of the Parmesan and the remaining oil. Allow the risotto to rest for 3–4 minutes before serving in a warmed bowl. Sprinkle a little of the remaining Parmesan on top and hand the rest separately. Add a grinding of black pepper to each portion and serve at once.

risotto with ricotta & basil

THIS IS A **WELL-FLAVOURED** RISOTTO, WHICH BENEFITS FROM THE DISTINCT **PUNGENCY** OF **BASIL**, MELLOWED WITH SMOOTH **RICOTTA**.

method

SERVES 3–4

1 Heat the oil in a large saucepan or flameproof casserole and fry the onion over a gentle heat until soft.

2 Tip in the rice. Cook for a few minutes, stirring, until the rice is coated with oil and is slightly translucent.

3 Pour in about a quarter of the stock. Cook, stirring, until all the stock has been absorbed, then add another ladleful. Continue in this manner, adding more stock when the previous ladleful has been absorbed, until the risotto has been cooking for about 20 minutes and the rice is just tender.

4 Spoon the ricotta into a bowl and break it up a little with a fork. Stir into the risotto along with the basil and Parmesan. Taste and adjust the seasoning, then cover and let stand for 2–3 minutes before serving, garnished with basil leaves.

ingredients

45ml/3 tbsp **olive oil**
1 **onion**, finely chopped
275g/10oz/1½ cups **risotto rice**
1 litre/1¾ pints/4 cups hot **chicken** or **vegetable stock**
175g/6oz/¾ cup **ricotta cheese**
50g/2oz/generous 1 cup fresh **basil** leaves, finely chopped, plus extra to garnish
75g/3oz/1 cup freshly grated **Parmesan cheese**
salt and freshly ground **black pepper**

risotto with four cheeses

THIS IS A **VERY RICH** DISH. SERVE IT FOR A SPECIAL **DINNER-PARTY** FIRST COURSE, WITH A LIGHT, DRY **SPARKLING WHITE WINE**.

method

SERVES 4

1 Melt the butter in a large, heavy-based saucepan or deep frying pan and fry the onion over a gentle heat for about 4–5 minutes, stirring frequently, until softened and lightly browned. Pour the stock into another pan and heat it to simmering point.

2 Add the rice to the onion mixture, stir until the grains start to swell and burst, then add the wine. Stir until it stops sizzling and most of it has been absorbed by the rice, then pour in a little of the hot stock. Add salt and pepper to taste. Stir over a low heat until the stock has been absorbed.

3 Gradually add the remaining stock, a little at a time, allowing the rice to absorb the liquid before adding more, and stirring constantly. After 20–25 minutes the rice will be *al dente* and the risotto creamy.

4 Turn off the heat under the pan, then add the Gruyère, taleggio, Gorgonzola and 30ml/2 tbsp of the Parmesan cheese. Stir gently until the cheeses have melted, then taste for seasoning. Spoon into a serving bowl and garnish with parsley. Serve the remaining Parmesan separately.

ingredients

40g/1½oz/3 tbsp **butter**

1 small **onion**, finely chopped

1.2 litres/2 pints/5 cups **chicken stock**, preferably home-made

350g/12oz/1¾ cups **risotto rice**

200ml/7fl oz/scant 1cup **dry white wine**

50g/2oz/½ cup grated **Gruyère cheese**

50g/2oz/½ cup diced **taleggio cheese**

50g/2oz/½ cup diced **Gorgonzola cheese**

50g/2oz/⅔ cup freshly grated **Parmesan cheese**

salt and freshly ground **black pepper**

chopped fresh **flat leaf parsley**, to garnish

THESE **DEEP FRIED** BALLS OF RISOTTO GO BY THE NAME OF **SUPPLI AL TELEFONO** IN THEIR NATIVE ITALY. STUFFED WITH **MOZZARELLA** CHEESE, THEY ARE VERY POPULAR **SNACKS**, WHICH IS HARDLY SURPRISING AS THEY ARE QUITE **DELICIOUS**.

ingredients

1 quantity **Risotto with Parmesan** or **Risotto with Mushrooms**

3 **eggs**

breadcrumbs and **plain flour**, to coat

115g/4oz/2/3 cup **mozzarella cheese**, cut into small cubes

oil, for deep frying

dressed **curly endive** and **cherry tomatoes**, to serve

fried rice balls stuffed with mozzarella

method

SERVES 4

1 Put the risotto in a bowl and allow it to cool completely. Beat two of the eggs, and stir them into the cold risotto until well mixed.

2 Use your hands to form the rice mixture into balls the size of a large egg. If the mixture is too moist to hold its shape well, stir in a few tablespoons of breadcrumbs.

3 Poke a hole into the centre of each ball with your finger, then fill it with a few small cubes of mozzarella, and close the hole over again with the rice mixture.

4 Heat the oil for deep frying until a small piece of bread sizzles as soon as it is dropped in.

5 Spread some flour on a plate. Beat the remaining egg in a shallow bowl. Sprinkle another plate with breadcrumbs. Roll the balls in the flour, then in the egg, and finally in the breadcrumbs. Fry them a few at a time in the hot oil until golden and crisp. Drain on kitchen paper while the remaining balls are being fried. Serve hot, with a simple salad of dressed curly endive leaves and cherry tomatoes.

cook's tip
Fried rice balls provide the perfect solution for using up leftover risotto, as they are best made with a cold mixture of risotto, cooked the day before.

vegetarian

THIS MAKES
AN **EXCELLENT**
VEGETARIAN **SUPPER**
DISH, OR A **STARTER**
FOR SIX.

ingredients

1 **red pepper**

1 **yellow pepper**

15ml/1 tbsp **olive oil**

25g/1oz/2 tbsp **butter**

1 **onion**, chopped

2 **garlic** cloves, crushed

275g/10oz/1½ cups **risotto rice**

1 litre/1¾ pints/4 cups simmering **vegetable stock**

50g/2oz/⅔ cup freshly grated **Parmesan cheese**

salt and freshly ground **black pepper**

freshly grated **Parmesan cheese**, to serve (optional)

roasted pepper risotto

method

SERVES 3–4

1 Preheat the grill to high. Cut the peppers in half, remove the seeds and pith and arrange, cut side down, on a baking sheet. Place under the grill for 5–6 minutes until the skin is charred. Put the peppers in a plastic bag, tie the ends and leave for 4–5 minutes.

2 Peel the peppers when they are cool enough to handle and the steam has loosened the skin. Cut into thin strips.

3 Heat the oil and butter in a pan and fry the onion and garlic for 4–5 minutes over a low heat until the onion begins to soften. Add the peppers and cook the mixture for 3–4 minutes more, stirring occasionally.

4 Stir in the rice. Cook over a medium heat for 3–4 minutes, stirring all the time, until the rice is evenly coated in oil and the outer part of each grain has become translucent.

5 Add a ladleful of stock. Cook, stirring, until all the liquid has been absorbed. Continue to add the stock, a ladleful at a time, making sure each quantity has been absorbed before adding the next.

6 When the rice is tender but retains a bit of "bite", stir in the Parmesan, and add seasoning to taste. Cover and leave to stand for 3–4 minutes, then serve, with extra Parmesan, if using.

pepper & courgette risotto with vermouth

ALL IT TAKES IS A LITTLE **TIME** AND **PATIENCE** TO CREATE THIS **SUPERB** RISOTTO.

method

SERVES 4

1 Pour the stock into a saucepan. Bring it to the boil, then reduce it to a low simmer.

2 Heat the oil in a large, shallow pan. Fry the onion until soft, then add the garlic and continue cooking for 1 minute more.

3 Stir in the rice until the grains are coated in the oil. Cook for 2 minutes, then add a small ladleful of the simmering stock and cook until it has been absorbed, stirring constantly.

4 Add the courgettes and green pepper to the pan. Cook for 1–2 minutes, then add another ladleful of stock. Stir until it has been absorbed. Continue adding stock in this way until all the stock has been added and the rice is *al dente*.

5 Stir in the vermouth, then the cheese. Season, then set aside to rest for 3–4 minutes. Serve, topped with Parmesan shavings.

ingredients

1 litre/1³/4 pints/4 cups
  vegetable stock
30ml/2 tbsp **olive oil**
1 **onion**, chopped
2 **garlic** cloves, crushed
250g/9oz/1¹/4 cups **risotto rice**
2 **courgettes**, chopped
1 **green pepper**, seeded and
  chopped
30ml/2 tbsp dry **white vermouth**
50g/2oz/²/3 cup freshly grated
  Parmesan cheese
salt and freshly ground **black
  pepper**
shavings of **Parmesan cheese**,
  to serve

risotto with asparagus

FRESH FARM **ASPARAGUS** ONLY HAS A SHORT SEASON, SO IT IS SENSIBLE TO MAKE THE MOST OF IT. THIS **ELEGANT** RISOTTO IS ABSOLUTELY **DELICIOUS**.

method

SERVES 3–4

1 Bring a pan of water to the boil. Cut off any woody pieces on the ends of the asparagus stalks, peel the lower portions, then cook in the water for 5 minutes. Drain the asparagus, reserving the cooking water, refresh under cold water and drain again. Cut the asparagus diagonally into 4cm/1½in pieces. Keep the tip and next-highest sections separate from the stalks.

2 Place the stock in a saucepan and add 450ml/¾ pint/scant 2 cups of the asparagus cooking water. Heat to simmering point, and keep it hot.

3 Melt two-thirds of the butter in a large, heavy-based saucepan or deep frying pan. Add the onion and fry until it is soft and golden. Stir in all the asparagus except the top two sections. Cook for 2–3 minutes. Add the rice and cook for 1–2 minutes, mixing well to coat it with butter. Stir in a ladleful of the hot liquid. Using a wooden spoon, stir until the stock has been absorbed.

4 Gradually add the remaining stock, a little at a time, allowing the rice to absorb the liquid before adding more, and stirring all the time.

5 After 10 minutes, add the remaining asparagus sections. Continue to cook as before, for about 15 minutes, until the rice is *al dente* and the risotto is creamy. Off the heat, stir in the remaining butter and the Parmesan. Grind in a little black pepper, and taste again for salt. Serve at once.

ingredients

225g/8oz fresh **asparagus**
750ml/1¼ pints/3 cups
   vegetable stock
65g/2½oz/5 tbsp **butter**
1 small **onion**, finely chopped
275g/10oz/1½ cups **risotto**
   rice, such as Arborio or
   Carnaroli
75g/3oz/1 cup freshly grated
   Parmesan cheese
salt and freshly ground **black**
   pepper

WILD **MUSHROOMS**
GIVE THIS
VEGETARIAN RISOTTO
A WONDERFUL
FLAVOUR.

ingredients

25g/1oz/4 tbsp dried **wild**
   mushrooms, preferably porcini
350ml/12fl oz/1^1/2 cups warm
   water
900ml/1^1/2 pints/3^3/4 cups
   vegetable stock
175g/6oz/1^1/2–2 cups **button**
   mushrooms, thinly sliced
juice of ^{1}/2 **lemon**
75g/3oz/6 tbsp **butter**
30ml/2 tbsp finely chopped fresh
   parsley
30ml/2 tbsp **olive oil**
1 small **onion**, finely chopped
275g/10oz/1^1/2 cups **risotto rice**
120ml/4fl oz/^{1}/2 cup **dry white**
   wine
45ml/3 tbsp freshly grated
   Parmesan cheese
salt and freshly ground **black**
   pepper
fresh **parsley** sprig, to garnish

risotto
with mushrooms

method
SERVES 3–4

1 Put the dried mushrooms in a bowl and add the warm water. Soak for at least 40 minutes, then lift them out and rinse them thoroughly. Filter the soaking water through a strainer lined with kitchen paper, then pour it into a pan. Add the stock and bring to simmering point.

2 Toss the button mushrooms with the lemon juice in a large, heavy-based pan. Melt a third of the butter. Stir in the button mushrooms and cook until they begin to brown. Stir in the fresh parsley, cook for 30 seconds more, then transfer to a bowl.

3 Heat the olive oil and half the remaining butter in the saucepan and fry the onion until soft and golden. Add the rice, stirring for 1–2 minutes to coat the grains.

4 Stir in all the mushrooms, add the wine and cook over a medium heat until it has been absorbed. Add the stock and mushroom soaking liquid a ladleful at a time, making sure each addition has been absorbed before you add more.

5 When all the liquid has been absorbed and the rice is *al dente*, add the remaining butter and the cheese. Season to taste, cover and set aside for 3–4 minutes before serving, garnished with fresh parsley.

THIS **VARIATION** ON THE CLASSIC RISOTTO ALLA MILANESE INCLUDES **SAFFRON**, **PORCINI** MUSHROOMS AND **PARMESAN**.

ingredients

15g/1/2oz/2 tbsp dried **porcini mushrooms**

150ml/1/4 pint/2/3 cup warm **water**

1 litre/13/4 pints/4 cups **vegetable stock**

generous pinch of **saffron strands**

30ml/2 tbsp **olive oil**

1 **onion**, finely chopped

1 **garlic** clove, crushed

350g/12oz/13/4 cups **Arborio** or **Carnaroli rice**

150ml/1/4 pint/2/3 cup **dry white wine**

25g/1oz/2 tbsp **butter**

50g/2oz/2/3 cup freshly grated **Parmesan cheese**

salt and freshly ground **black pepper**

pink and **yellow oyster mushrooms**, to serve (optional)

porcini & parmesan risotto

method

SERVES 3–4

1 Put the dried porcini in a bowl and pour over the warm water. Leave the mushrooms to soak for 20 minutes, then lift out with a slotted spoon. Filter the soaking water through a layer of kitchen paper in a sieve, then place it in a saucepan with the stock. Bring the liquid to a gentle simmer.

2 Spoon about 45ml/3 tbsp of the hot stock into a cup and stir in the saffron strands. Set aside. Finely chop the porcini.

3 Heat the oil in a separate pan and lightly sauté the onion, garlic and mushrooms for 5 minutes. Gradually add the rice, stirring to coat the grains in oil. Cook for 2 minutes, stirring constantly. Season with salt and pepper.

4 Pour in the white wine. Cook, stirring, until it has been absorbed, then ladle in a quarter of the stock. Cook, stirring, until the stock has been absorbed. Gradually add the remaining stock, a little at a time, allowing the rice to absorb the liquid before adding more, and stirring constantly.

5 After about 20 minutes, when all the stock has been absorbed and the rice is cooked but still has a "bite", stir in the butter, saffron water (with the strands) and half the Parmesan. Serve, sprinkled with the remaining Parmesan. Garnish with pink and yellow oyster mushrooms, if you like.

brown rice risotto with mushrooms & parmesan

A **CLASSIC** RISOTTO OF MIXED **MUSHROOMS**, HERBS AND FRESH **PARMESAN** CHEESE, BUT MADE USING BROWN **LONG GRAIN** RICE.

method

SERVES 3–4

1 Heat the oil in a large saucepan, add the shallots and garlic and cook gently for 5 minutes, stirring.

2 Drain the porcini, reserving their liquid, and chop roughly. Add the brown rice to the shallot mixture and stir to coat the grains in oil.

3 Stir the vegetable stock and the porcini soaking liquid into the rice mixture in the saucepan. Bring to the boil, lower the heat and simmer, uncovered, for about 20 minutes or until most of the liquid has been absorbed, stirring frequently.

4 Add all the mushrooms, stir well, and cook the risotto for 10–15 minutes more until the liquid has been absorbed.

5 Season with salt and pepper to taste, stir in the chopped parsley and grated Parmesan and serve at once.

ingredients

15ml/1 tbsp **olive oil**

4 **shallots**, finely chopped

2 **garlic** cloves, crushed

15g/^{1}/2oz/2 tbsp dried **porcini mushrooms**, soaked in 150ml/^{1}/4 pint/^{2}/3 cup hot **water** for 20 minutes

250g/9oz/1^1/3 cups **brown long grain rice**

900ml/1^1/2 pints/3^3/4 cups well-flavoured **vegetable stock**

450g/1lb/6 cups **mixed mushrooms**, such as closed cup, chestnut and field mushrooms, sliced if large

30–45ml/2–3 tbsp chopped fresh **flat leaf parsley**

50g/2oz/^{2}/3 cup freshly grated **Parmesan cheese**

salt and freshly ground **black pepper**

rosemary risotto with borlotti beans

THIS IS A CLASSIC RISOTTO WITH A **SUBTLE** AND **COMPLEX** TASTE, FROM THE HEADY FLAVOURS OF **ROSEMARY** TO THE SAVOURY BEANS AND THE **FRUITY-SWEET** FLAVOURS OF MASCARPONE AND PARMESAN.

method

SERVES 3–4

1 Drain the beans, rinse under cold water and drain again. Purée about two-thirds of the beans fairly coarsely in a food processor or blender. Set the remaining beans aside.

2 Heat the olive oil in a large pan and gently fry the onion and garlic for 6–8 minutes until very soft. Add the rice and cook over a medium heat for a few minutes, stirring constantly, until the grains are thoroughly coated in oil and are slightly translucent.

3 Pour in the wine. Cook over a medium heat for 2–3 minutes, stirring all the time, until the wine has been absorbed. Add the stock gradually, a ladleful at a time, waiting for each quantity to be absorbed before adding more, and continuing to stir.

4 When the rice is three-quarters cooked, stir in the bean purée. Continue to cook the risotto, adding the remaining stock, until it is creamy and the rice is tender but still has a bit of "bite". Add the reserved beans, with the mascarpone, Parmesan and rosemary, then season to taste. Stir thoroughly, then cover and leave to stand for about 5 minutes so that the risotto absorbs the flavours fully and the rice completes cooking. Serve with extra Parmesan, if you like.

ingredients

400g/14oz can **borlotti beans**
30ml/2 tbsp **olive oil**
1 **onion**, chopped
2 **garlic** cloves, crushed
275g/10oz/1 1/2 cups **risotto rice**
175ml/6fl oz/3/4 cup **dry white wine**
900ml–1 litre/1 1/2–1 3/4 pints/3 3/4–4 cups simmering **vegetable stock**
60ml/4 tbsp **mascarpone cheese**
65g/2 1/2oz/scant 1 cup freshly grated **Parmesan cheese**, plus extra, to serve (optional)
5ml/1 tsp chopped fresh **rosemary**
salt and freshly ground **black pepper**

variation

Fresh thyme or marjoram could be used for this risotto instead of rosemary, if preferred. One of the great virtues of risotto is that it lends itself well to variations. Experiment with different herbs to make your own speciality dish.

AUBERGINES ARE A **CHALLENGE** TO THE CREATIVE COOK AND ALLOW FOR SOME **UNUSUAL** RECIPE IDEAS. HERE, THEY ARE FILLED WITH A RICE STUFFING AND **BAKED** WITH A CHEESE AND **PINE NUT** TOPPING.

ingredients

4 small **aubergines**

105ml/7 tbsp **olive oil**

1 small **onion**, chopped

175g/6oz/scant 1 cup **risotto rice**

750ml/1¼ pints/3 cups hot **vegetable stock**

15ml/1 tbsp **white wine vinegar**

25g/1oz/⅓ cup freshly grated **Parmesan cheese**

15g/½oz/2 tbsp **pine nuts**

For the tomato sauce

300ml/½ pint/1¼ cups thick **passata** or **puréed tomatoes**

5ml/1 tsp **mild curry paste**

pinch of **salt**

risotto-stuffed aubergines with spicy tomato sauce

method

SERVES 4

1 Preheat the oven to 200°C/400°F/Gas 6. Cut the aubergines in half lengthways, and remove the flesh with a small knife. Brush the shells with 30ml/2 tbsp of the oil and bake on a baking sheet, supported by crumpled foil, for 6–8 minutes.

2 Chop the aubergine flesh. Heat the remaining oil in a medium pan. Add the aubergine flesh and the onion, and cook over a gentle heat for 3–4 minutes until soft. Add the rice and stock, and leave to simmer, uncovered, for about 15 minutes. Add the vinegar.

3 Increase the oven temperature to 230°C/450°F/Gas 8. Spoon the rice mixture into the aubergine skins, top with the cheese and pine nuts, return to the oven and brown for 5 minutes.

4 To make the sauce, mix the passata or puréed tomatoes with the curry paste in a small pan. Heat through and add salt to taste. Spoon the sauce on to four individual serving plates and arrange two aubergine halves on each one.

cook's tip
If the aubergine shells do not stand level, cut a thin slice from the bottom.

ingredients

115g/4oz/1 cup shelled fresh **peas**

115g/4oz/1 cup **green beans**, cut into short lengths

30ml/2 tbsp **olive oil**

75g/3oz/6 tbsp **butter**

1 **acorn squash**, skin and seeds removed, flesh cut into matchsticks

1 **onion**, finely chopped

275g/10oz/1½ cups **risotto rice**

120ml/4fl oz/½ cup Italian **dry white vermouth**

1 litre/1¾ pints/4 cups boiling **vegetable stock**

75g/3oz/1 cup freshly grated **Parmesan cheese**

salt and freshly ground **black pepper**

variation

Shelled broad beans can be used instead of the peas, and asparagus tips instead of the green beans. Use courgettes if acorn squash is not available.

risotto with four vegetables

method

SERVES 3–4

1 Bring a saucepan of lightly salted water to the boil, add the peas and beans and cook for 2–3 minutes, until the vegetables are just tender. Drain, refresh under cold running water, drain again and set aside.

2 Heat the oil with 25g/1oz/2 tbsp of the butter in a medium saucepan until foaming. Add the squash and cook gently for 2–3 minutes or until just softened. Remove with a slotted spoon and set aside. Add the onion to the pan and cook gently for about 3 minutes, stirring frequently, until softened.

3 Stir in the rice until the grains start to swell and burst, then add the vermouth. Stir until the vermouth stops sizzling and most of it has been absorbed by the rice, then add a few ladlefuls of the stock, with salt and pepper to taste. Stir over a low heat until the stock has been absorbed.

4 Gradually add the remaining stock, a few ladlefuls at a time, allowing the rice to absorb the liquid before adding more, and stirring all the time.

5 After about 20 minutes, when all the stock has been absorbed and the rice is cooked and creamy but still has a "bite", gently stir in the vegetables, the remaining butter and about half the grated Parmesan. Heat through, then taste for seasoning and serve with the remaining grated Parmesan served separately.

lentil risotto with vegetables

THIS ISN'T A **TRUE** RISOTTO, AS THE LIQUID IS ADDED ALL AT ONCE, BUT THE **COMBINATION** OF LENTILS AND BASMATI RICE WORKS VERY WELL, ESPECIALLY WHEN **COLOURFUL** FRESH **VEGETABLES** ARE STIRRED IN AT THE END OF THE COOKING TIME.

method

SERVES 4

1 Pour the stock into a pan, bring it to the boil, then reduce it to simmering point.

2 Heat the oil in a wide pan and gently fry the onion, garlic and carrot for 5–6 minutes, until the onion is transparent and the carrot has softened slightly.

3 Drain the rice and lentils and add both to the pan, with the cumin, cinnamon, cardamom seeds and cloves. Fry over a low heat for 5 minutes more, stirring well to prevent the mixture from sticking to the bottom of the pan.

4 Pour in all the stock and bring to the boil, then cover the pan and simmer very gently for 15 minutes, or until the liquid has been absorbed and the rice and lentils are tender. The mixture should still be quite moist. Season to taste.

5 Add the celery, avocado and tomatoes to the rice and lentil mixture, and stir gently to mix. Spoon the mixture into a large serving bowl and serve immediately.

ingredients

600ml/1 pint/2^1/$_2$ cups
   vegetable stock

45ml/3 tbsp **sunflower oil**

1 large **onion**, thinly sliced

2 **garlic** cloves, crushed

1 large **carrot**, cut into matchsticks

225g/8oz/generous 1 cup
   basmati rice, soaked for
   30 minutes in cold water

115g/4oz/^{1}/$_2$ cup green or brown
   lentils, soaked overnight in
   cold water

5ml/1 tsp ground **cumin**

5ml/1 tsp ground **cinnamon**

20 black **cardamom seeds**

6 **cloves**

2 **celery** sticks, thinly sliced

1 large **avocado**, peeled, stoned
   and diced

3 **plum tomatoes**, diced

salt and freshly ground **black
   pepper**

variation

Other seasonal vegetables could be used for this risotto. In the summer try diced courgettes, aubergine or sweet red pepper. Winter options could include pumpkin, broccoli or leeks.

jerusalem artichoke risotto

THIS IS A **SIMPLE** AND **WARMING** RISOTTO, WHICH BENEFITS FROM THE ADDITION OF THE **DELICIOUS** AND **DISTINCTIVE** FLAVOUR OF JERUSALEM **ARTICHOKES**.

method

SERVES 3–4

1 Peel the artichokes, cut them into pieces and immediately add them to a pan of lightly salted water. Simmer them until tender, then drain and mash with 15g/½oz/1 tbsp of the butter. Add a little more salt, if needed.

2 Heat the oil and the remaining butter in a pan and fry the onion and garlic for 5–6 minutes until soft. Add the rice and cook over a medium heat for about 2 minutes until the grains are translucent around the edges.

3 Pour in the wine, stir until it has been absorbed, then start adding the simmering stock, a ladleful at a time, making sure each quantity has been absorbed before adding more.

4 When you have just one last ladleful of stock to add, stir in the mashed artichokes and the chopped thyme. Season with salt and pepper. Continue cooking until the risotto is creamy and the artichokes are hot. Stir in the Parmesan. Remove from the heat, cover the pan and leave the risotto to stand for a few minutes. Spoon into a serving dish, garnish with thyme, and serve with Parmesan cheese.

ingredients

400g/14oz **Jerusalem artichokes**
40g/1½oz/3 tbsp **butter**
15ml/1 tbsp **olive oil**
1 **onion**, finely chopped
1 **garlic** clove, crushed
275g/10oz/1½ cups **risotto rice**
120ml/4fl oz/½ cup **fruity white wine**
1 litre/1¾ pints/4 cups simmering **vegetable stock**
10ml/2 tsp chopped fresh **thyme**
40g/1½oz/½ cup freshly grated **Parmesan cheese**, plus extra, to serve
salt and freshly ground **black pepper**
fresh **thyme** sprigs, to garnish

THIS **COLOURFUL** RISOTTO LOOKS **STUNNING** WHEN SERVED IN COOKED **SQUASH** HALVES.

ingredients

1.2 litres/2 pints/5 cups **vegetable stock**
40g/1^1/2oz/3 tbsp **butter**
1 small **onion**, chopped
50g/2oz peeled and coarsely grated **acorn squash** or **pumpkin**
250g/9oz/1^1/4 cups **risotto rice**
1 **courgette**, quartered lengthways and chopped
150g/5oz/1^1/4 cups frozen **peas**, thawed
40g/1^1/2oz/^{1}/2 cup freshly grated **Parmesan cheese**
salt and freshly ground **black pepper**
cooked **acorn squash** halves, hollowed out, to serve (optional)

green & orange risotto

method

SERVES 3–4

1 Bring the stock to the boil in a saucepan and reduce it to a low simmer.

2 Melt one-third of the butter in a heavy-based saucepan or casserole. Add the onion and cook for about 5 minutes, until softened. Add the grated squash or pumpkin and cook for 1 minute, stirring.

3 Add the rice and stir to coat all the grains well. Cook for 1 minute over a medium heat, stirring, then add a small ladleful of the hot stock. Cook until it has been absorbed, stirring constantly.

4 Gradually add the remaining stock, a little at a time, allowing the rice to absorb the liquid before adding more, and stirring constantly. After about 5 minutes, stir in the courgette pieces. After about 10 minutes, stir in the peas.

5 When the rice is *al dente* and the vegetables are tender, remove the pan from the heat. Add the remaining butter and the Parmesan and set aside to rest for 3–4 minutes. Season to taste. If you like, serve in hollowed-out acorn squash halves.

THIS MAY SEEM **EXTRAVAGANT**, BUT IT MAKES A REALLY BEAUTIFULLY **FLAVOURED** RISOTTO, PERFECT FOR A **SPECIAL** ANNIVERSARY DINNER.

ingredients

25g/1oz/2 tbsp **butter**

2 **shallots**, finely chopped

275g/10oz/1½ cups **risotto rice**, preferably Carnaroli

½ bottle or 300ml/½ pint/ 1¼ cups **champagne**

750ml/1¼ pints/3 cups simmering **light vegetable stock**

150ml/¼ pint/⅔ cup **double cream**

40g/1½oz/½ cup freshly grated **Parmesan cheese**

10ml/2 tsp very finely chopped fresh **chervil**

salt and freshly ground **black pepper**

black truffle shavings, to garnish (optional)

champagne risotto

method

SERVES 3–4

1 Melt the butter in a pan and fry the shallots for 2–3 minutes until softened. Add the rice and cook, stirring all the time, until the grains are evenly coated in butter and are beginning to look translucent around the edges.

2 Pour in about two-thirds of the champagne and cook over a high heat so that the liquid bubbles fiercely. Cook, stirring, until all the liquid has been absorbed before beginning to add the hot stock.

3 Add the stock, a ladleful at a time, making sure that each addition has been completely absorbed before adding the next. The risotto should gradually become creamy and velvety and all the stock should be absorbed.

4 When the rice is tender but retains a bit of "bite", stir in the remaining champagne and the double cream and Parmesan. Adjust the seasoning. Remove from the heat, cover and leave to stand for a few minutes. Stir in the chervil. If you want to gild the lily, garnish with a few truffle shavings.

pumpkin & pistachio risotto

VEGETARIANS TIRED OF THE STANDARD DINNER-PARTY FARE WILL LOVE THIS **ELEGANT** COMBINATION OF CREAMY, **GOLDEN** RICE AND **ORANGE** PUMPKIN. IT WOULD LOOK PARTICULARLY **IMPRESSIVE** SERVED IN THE HOLLOWED-OUT **PUMPKIN** SHELL.

method

SERVES 3–4

1 Bring the stock or water to the boil and reduce to a low simmer. Ladle a little of it into a small bowl. Add the saffron strands and leave to infuse.

2 Heat the oil in a large, heavy-based saucepan or deep frying pan. Add the onion and garlic and cook gently for about 5 minutes until softened. Add the pumpkin and rice and stir to coat everything in oil. Cook for a few more minutes until the rice looks transparent.

3 Pour in the wine and allow it to bubble hard. When it has been absorbed, add a quarter of the hot stock or water and the saffron liquid. Stir until all the liquid has been absorbed. Gradually add the remaining stock or water, a little at a time, allowing the rice to absorb the liquid before adding more, and stirring constantly. After 20–30 minutes the rice should be golden yellow, creamy and *al dente*.

4 Stir in the Parmesan cheese, cover the pan and leave the risotto to stand for 5 minutes. To finish, stir in the pistachios and marjoram or oregano. Season to taste with a little salt, nutmeg and pepper, scatter over a few marjoram or oregano leaves and serve.

ingredients

1.2 litres/2 pints/5 cups **vegetable stock** or **water**

generous pinch of **saffron strands**

30ml/2 tbsp **olive oil**

1 **onion**, chopped

2 **garlic** cloves, crushed

900g/2lb **pumpkin**, peeled, seeded and cut into 2cm/ ¾in cubes (about 7 cups)

400g/14oz/2 cups **risotto rice**

200ml/7fl oz/scant 1 cup **dry white wine**

30ml/2 tbsp freshly grated **Parmesan cheese**

50g/2oz/½ cup **pistachios**, coarsely chopped

45ml/3 tbsp chopped fresh **marjoram** or **oregano**, plus leaves to garnish

salt, freshly grated **nutmeg** and freshly ground **black pepper**

spinach & rice soup

USE VERY **YOUNG** SPINACH LEAVES TO
PREPARE THIS **LIGHT** AND **FRESH-TASTING**
SOUP, AND SERVE WITH **PARMESAN** SHAVINGS.

method

SERVES 4

1 Place the spinach in a large pan with just the water that clings to its leaves after washing. Add a large pinch of salt. Heat gently until the spinach has wilted, then remove from the heat and drain, reserving any liquid.

2 Either chop the spinach finely using a large kitchen knife or place in a food processor and process the leaves to a fairly coarse purée.

3 Heat the oil in a large saucepan and gently cook the onion, garlic and chilli for 4–5 minutes until softened. Stir in the rice until well coated, then pour in the stock and reserved spinach liquid. Bring to the boil, lower the heat and simmer for 10 minutes.

4 Add the spinach, with salt and pepper to taste. Cook for 5–7 minutes, until the rice is tender. Check the seasoning. Serve in heated bowls, topped with the shavings of cheese.

---

cook's tip

Buy Parmesan or Pecorino cheese in the piece from a reputable supplier, and it will be full of flavour and easy to grate or shave with a vegetable peeler.

ingredients

675g/1 1/2lb fresh **spinach leaves**, washed

45ml/3 tbsp extra virgin **olive oil**

1 small **onion**, finely chopped

2 **garlic** cloves, finely chopped

1 small fresh **red chilli**, seeded and finely chopped

225g/8oz/generous 1 cup **risotto rice**

1.2 litres/2 pints/5 cups **vegetable stock**

salt and freshly ground **black pepper**

shavings of pared **Parmesan** or **Pecorino cheese**, to serve

THIS MAKES A DELIGHTFUL **LIGHT** LUNCH. COOK EACH **FRITTATA** SEPARATELY, AND PREFERABLY IN A SMALL, **CAST IRON** PAN, SO THAT THE **EGGS** COOK QUICKLY UNDERNEATH BUT STAY **MOIST** ON TOP.

ingredients

30–45ml/2–3 tbsp **olive oil**

1 small **onion**, finely chopped

1 **garlic** clove, crushed

1 large **red pepper**, seeded and cut into thin strips

150g/5oz/¾ cup **risotto rice**

400–475ml/14–16fl oz/ 1⅔–2 cups simmering **vegetable stock**

25–40g/1–1½oz/2–3 tbsp **butter**

175g/6oz/2½ cups **button mushrooms**, finely sliced

60ml/4 tbsp freshly grated **Parmesan cheese**

6–8 **eggs**

salt and freshly ground **black pepper**

risotto frittata

method

SERVES 4

1 Heat 15ml/1 tbsp oil in a large frying pan and fry the onion and garlic over a gentle heat for 2–3 minutes until the onion begins to soften but does not brown. Add the pepper and cook, stirring, for 4–5 minutes, until soft.

2 Stir in the rice and cook gently for 2–3 minutes, stirring all the time, until the grains are evenly coated with oil.

3 Add a quarter of the vegetable stock and season. Stir over a low heat until the stock has been absorbed. Continue to add more stock, a little at a time, allowing the rice to absorb the liquid before adding more. Continue cooking in this way until the rice is *al dente*.

4 In a separate small pan, heat a little of the remaining oil and some butter and quickly fry the mushrooms until golden. Transfer to a plate.

5 When the rice is tender, remove from the heat and stir in the mushrooms and Parmesan cheese.

6 Beat together the eggs with 40ml/8 tsp cold water and season well. Heat the remaining oil and butter in an omelette pan and add the risotto mixture. Spread the mixture out in the pan, then immediately add the beaten egg, tilting the pan so that the omelette cooks evenly. Fry over a moderately high heat for 1–2 minutes, then transfer to a warmed plate and serve.

cook's tip
This will make a more substantial dish for two, using five or six eggs. If preferred, the frittata could be cooked as individual portions.

meat & poultry

THIS **DELICIOUS** RISOTTO MAKES A **HEALTHY** AND **FILLING** MEAL, SERVED WITH COOKED FRESH **SEASONAL** VEGETABLES OR A MIXED **GREEN** SALAD.

ingredients

15ml/1 tbsp **olive oil**

1 **onion**, chopped

2 **garlic** cloves, finely chopped

175g/6oz **smoked pancetta**, diced

350g/12oz/1¾ cups **risotto rice**

1.5 litres/2½ pints/6¼ cups simmering **chicken stock**

225g/8oz/2 cups frozen **baby broad beans**

30ml/2 tbsp chopped fresh **mixed herbs**, such as parsley, thyme and oregano

salt and freshly ground **black pepper**

shavings of **Parmesan cheese**, to serve

pancetta & broad bean risotto

method

SERVES 4

1 Heat the oil in a large saucepan. Add the onion, garlic and pancetta and cook gently for about 5 minutes, stirring occasionally. Do not allow the onion and garlic to brown.

2 Add the rice to the pan and cook for 1 minute, stirring. Add a ladleful of stock and cook, stirring all the time, until the liquid has been absorbed.

3 Continue adding the stock, a ladleful at a time, until the rice is tender, and almost all the liquid has been absorbed. This will take 30–35 minutes.

4 Meanwhile, cook the broad beans in a saucepan of lightly salted, boiling water for about 3 minutes until tender. Drain well and stir into the risotto, with the mixed herbs. Add salt and pepper to taste. Spoon into a bowl and serve, sprinkled with shavings of fresh Parmesan cheese.

cook's tip
If the broad beans are large, or if you prefer skinned beans, remove the outer skin after cooking.

risotto with smoked bacon & tomato

A **CLASSIC** RISOTTO, WITH PLENTY OF **ONIONS**, SMOKED BACON AND SUN-DRIED TOMATOES. YOU'LL WANT TO **KEEP GOING BACK** FOR MORE!

method

SERVES 4

1 Drain the sun-dried tomatoes and reserve 15ml/1 tbsp of the oil. Roughly chop the tomatoes and set aside. Cut the bacon into 2.5cm/1in pieces.

2 Heat the oil from the sun-dried tomatoes in a large saucepan. Fry the bacon until well cooked and golden. Remove with a slotted spoon and drain on kitchen paper.

3 Heat 25g/1oz/2 tbsp of the butter in a saucepan and fry the onions and garlic over a medium heat for 10 minutes, until soft and golden brown.

4 Stir in the rice. Cook for 1 minute, until the grains turn translucent. Stir the wine into the stock. Add a ladleful of the mixture to the rice and cook gently until the liquid has been absorbed.

5 Stir in another ladleful of the stock and wine mixture and allow it to be absorbed. Repeat this process until all the liquid has been used up. This should take 25–30 minutes. The risotto will turn thick and creamy, and the rice should be tender but not sticky.

6 Just before serving, stir in the bacon, sun-dried tomatoes, Parmesan, half the herbs and the remaining butter. Adjust the seasoning (remember that the bacon may be quite salty) and serve sprinkled with the remaining herbs.

ingredients

8 **sun-dried tomatoes** in olive oil

275g/10oz good-quality rindless **smoked back bacon**

75g/3oz/6 tbsp **butter**

450g/1lb **onions**, roughly chopped

2 **garlic** cloves, crushed

350g/12oz/1¾ cups **risotto rice**

300ml/½ pint/1¼ cups **dry white wine**

1 litre/1¾ pints/4 cups simmering **vegetable stock**

50g/2oz/⅔ cup freshly grated **Parmesan cheese**

45ml/3 tbsp mixed chopped fresh **chives** and **flat leaf parsley**

salt and freshly ground **black pepper**

leek & ham risotto

ANOTHER **SIMPLE** RISOTTO THAT MAKES AN
EASY SUPPER, YET IS **SPECIAL** ENOUGH FOR
A DINNER PARTY.

ingredients

7.5ml/1½ tsp **olive oil**

40g/1½oz/3 tbsp **butter**

2 **leeks**, cut in slices

175g/6oz **prosciutto**, torn into
pieces

75g/3oz/generous 1 cup **button
mushrooms**, sliced

275g/10oz/1½ cups **risotto rice**

1 litre/1¾ pints/4 cups simmering
chicken stock

45ml/3 tbsp chopped fresh **flat
leaf parsley**

40g/1½oz/½ cup freshly grated
Parmesan cheese

salt and freshly ground **black
pepper**

method

SERVES 4

1 Heat the oil and butter in a pan and fry the leeks until soft. Set aside
a few strips of prosciutto for the garnish and add the rest to the pan.
Fry for 1 minute, then add the mushrooms and stir-fry for 2–3 minutes
until lightly browned.

2 Add the rice. Cook, stirring, for 1–2 minutes until the grains are evenly
coated in oil and have become translucent around the edges. Add a
ladleful of hot stock. Stir until this has been absorbed completely, then
add the next ladleful. Continue adding stock in this way until all the
liquid has been absorbed.

3 When the risotto is creamy and the rice is tender but still has a bit of
"bite", stir in the parsley and Parmesan. Adjust the seasoning, remove
from the heat and cover. Allow to rest for a few minutes. Spoon into a
bowl, garnish with the reserved prosciutto and serve.

rabbit & lemon grass risotto

THE **LEMON GRASS** ADDS A PLEASANT **TANG**
TO THIS RISOTTO. IF RABBIT ISN'T AVAILABLE,
USE **CHICKEN** OR **TURKEY** INSTEAD.

ingredients

225g/8oz **rabbit meat**, cut into
strips

seasoned flour

50g/2oz/4 tbsp **butter**

15ml/1 tbsp **olive oil**

45ml/3 tbsp **dry sherry**

1 **onion**, finely chopped

1 **garlic** clove, crushed

1 **lemon grass** stalk, peeled and
very finely sliced

275g/10oz/1½ cups **risotto
rice**, preferably Carnaroli

1 litre/1¾ pints/4 cups simmering
chicken stock

10ml/2 tsp chopped fresh **thyme**

45ml/3 tbsp **double cream**

25g/1oz/⅓ cup freshly grated
Parmesan cheese

salt and freshly ground **black
pepper**

method

SERVES 3–4

1 Coat the rabbit strips in the seasoned flour. Heat half the butter and
olive oil in a frying pan and fry the rabbit quickly until evenly brown.
Add the sherry, and allow to boil briefly to burn off the alcohol.
Season with salt and pepper and set aside.

2 Heat the remaining olive oil and butter in a large saucepan. Fry the
onion and garlic over a low heat for 4–5 minutes until the onion is
soft. Add the sliced lemon grass and cook for a few more minutes.

3 Add the rice and stir to coat in the oil. Add a ladleful of stock and
cook, stirring, until the liquid has been absorbed. Continue adding the
stock gradually, stirring constantly. When the rice is almost cooked,
stir in three-quarters of the rabbit strips, with the pan juices. Add the
thyme and seasoning.

4 Continue cooking until the rice is tender but still has a "bite". Stir in
the cream and Parmesan, remove from the heat and cover. Leave to
rest before serving, garnished with the reserved rabbit strips.

A CLASSIC **PEA** AND **HAM** RISOTTO FROM THE **VENETO**. ALTHOUGH THIS IS **TRADITIONALLY** SERVED AS A STARTER IN **ITALY**, IT ALSO MAKES AN **EXCELLENT** SUPPER DISH WITH HOT, **CRUSTY BREAD**.

ingredients

75g/3oz/6 tbsp **butter**

1 small **onion**, finely chopped

about 1 litre/1¾ pints/4 cups simmering **chicken stock**

275g/10oz/1½ cups **risotto rice**

150ml/¼ pint/⅔ cup **dry white wine**

225g/8oz/2 cups frozen **petits pois**, thawed

115g/4oz cooked **ham**, diced

salt and freshly ground **black pepper**

50g/2oz/⅔ cup freshly grated **Parmesan cheese**, to serve

risi e bisi

method

SERVES 4

1 Melt 50g/2oz/4 tbsp of the butter in a saucepan until foaming. Add the onion and cook gently for about 3 minutes, stirring frequently, until softened. Have the hot stock ready in an adjacent pan.

2 Add the rice to the onion mixture. Stir until the grains start to swell, then pour in the wine. Stir until it stops sizzling and most of it has been absorbed, then pour in a little hot stock, with salt and pepper to taste. Stir continuously, over a low heat, until all the stock has been absorbed.

3 Add the remaining stock, a little at a time, allowing the rice to absorb all the liquid before adding more, and stirring constantly. Add the peas after about 20 minutes. After 25–30 minutes, the rice should be *al dente* and the risotto moist and creamy.

4 Gently stir in the diced cooked ham and the remaining butter. Heat through until the butter has melted, then taste for seasoning. Transfer to a warmed serving bowl. Grate or shave a little Parmesan over the top and serve the rest separately.

---

cook's tip
Always use fresh Parmesan cheese, grated off a block. It has a far superior flavour to the ready-grated Parmesan.

---

risotto with chicken

THIS IS A CLASSIC **COMBINATION** OF CHICKEN AND RICE, COOKED WITH **PARMA HAM**, WHITE **WINE** AND **PARMESAN** CHEESE.

method

SERVES 6

1 Heat the oil in a frying pan over a moderately high heat. Add the chicken cubes and cook, stirring, until they start to turn white.

2 Reduce the heat to low and add the onion and garlic. Cook, stirring, until the onion is soft. Stir in the rice. Sauté for 1–2 minutes, stirring constantly, until all the rice grains are coated in oil.

3 Add the wine and cook, stirring, until the wine has been absorbed. Stir the saffron into the simmering stock, then add ladlefuls of stock to the rice, allowing each ladleful to be absorbed before adding the next.

4 When the rice is three-quarters cooked, add the Parma ham and continue cooking until the rice is just tender and the risotto creamy.

5 Add the butter and the Parmesan and stir in well. Season with salt and pepper to taste. Serve the risotto hot, sprinkled with a little more Parmesan, and garnish with parsley.

ingredients

30ml/2 tbsp **olive oil**

225g/8oz skinless, boneless **chicken breasts**, cut into 2.5cm/1in cubes

1 **onion**, finely chopped

1 **garlic** clove, finely chopped

450g/1lb/2⅓ cups **risotto rice**

120ml/4fl oz/½ cup **dry white wine**

1.5ml/¼ tsp **saffron threads**

1.75 litres/3 pints/7½ cups simmering **chicken stock**

50g/2oz **Parma ham**, cut into thin strips

25g/1oz/2 tbsp **butter**, cubed

25g/1oz/⅓ cup freshly grated **Parmesan cheese**, plus extra to serve

salt and freshly ground **black pepper**

flat leaf parsley, to garnish

chicken & vegetable risotto

A **COLOURFUL** RISOTTO COMBINING **PEPPERS**, **BEANS** AND **MUSHROOMS** WITH **CHICKEN**.

method

SERVES 4

1 Pour the stock into a saucepan, bring it to the boil, then reduce it to simmering point.

2 Heat the oil in a wide pan. Add the rice and stir until the grains are coated, then cook for 2 minutes, until transparent. Add the onion and minced chicken. Cook for 5 minutes, stirring occasionally.

3 Pour in the stock and bring to the boil. Stir in the red and yellow peppers and reduce the heat. Cook gently for 10 minutes.

4 Add the green beans and mushrooms and cook for 10 minutes more.

5 Stir in the chopped parsley and season well to taste. Cook for 10 minutes, or until all the liquid has been absorbed. Serve immediately, garnished with parsley sprigs.

ingredients

600ml/1 pint/2^1/$_2$ cups **chicken stock**

15ml/1 tbsp **oil**

200g/7oz/1 cup **risotto rice**

1 **onion**, chopped

225g/8oz uncooked **minced chicken**

1 **red pepper**, seeded and chopped

1 **yellow pepper**, seeded and chopped

75g/3oz frozen **green beans**, thawed

115g/4oz/scant 2 cups **chestnut mushrooms**, sliced

15ml/1 tbsp chopped fresh **parsley**

salt and freshly ground **black pepper**

fresh **parsley** sprigs, to garnish

NOT ALL RISOTTOS NEED TO BE WATCHED – AND STIRRED – ALL THE TIME. THIS SIMPLIFIED VERSION IS IDEAL FOR NERVOUS NOVICES.

ingredients

1 **onion**, chopped

2 **garlic** cloves, crushed

1 fresh **red chilli**, seeded and finely chopped

175g/6oz/1^1/2–2 cups **mushrooms**, sliced

2 **celery** sticks, chopped

200g/7oz/1 cup **long grain brown rice**

450ml/^{3}/4 pint/scant 2 cups **chicken stock**

150ml/^{1}/4 pint/^{2}/3 cup **white wine**

225g/8oz skinless, boneless **chicken breasts**

400g/14oz can red **kidney beans**, drained

200g/7oz can **sweetcorn** kernels, drained

115g/4oz/^{2}/3 cup **sultanas**

175g/6oz/1 cup small **broccoli** florets

30–45ml/2–3 tbsp chopped fresh **mixed herbs**

salt and freshly ground **black pepper**

chicken & bean risotto

method

SERVES 4

1 Put the onion, garlic, chilli, mushrooms, celery, rice, stock and wine in a saucepan. Bring to the boil, then lower the heat, cover and simmer for 15 minutes.

2 Dice the chicken. Add it to the rice mixture with the kidney beans, sweetcorn and sultanas. Cook for 20 minutes more, until all the liquid has been absorbed but the mixture is still moist.

3 Meanwhile, cook the broccoli in boiling water or a steamer for 5 minutes, then drain thoroughly. Stir the broccoli into the risotto. Add the chopped fresh herbs, season to taste and serve immediately.

stuffed chicken rolls

THESE **DELICIOUS** CHICKEN ROLLS ARE SIMPLE TO MAKE, BUT **SOPHISTICATED** ENOUGH TO SERVE AT A DINNER PARTY, ESPECIALLY IF YOU ARRANGE SLICES ON A **BED OF TAGLIATELLE** TOSSED WITH FRIED WILD **MUSHROOMS**.

ingredients

25g/1oz/2 tbsp **butter**

1 **garlic** clove, chopped

150g/5oz/1¼ cups cooked **risotto rice**

45ml/3 tbsp **ricotta cheese**

10ml/2 tsp chopped fresh **flat leaf parsley**

5ml/1 tsp chopped fresh **tarragon**

4 skinless, boneless **chicken breasts**

3–4 slices **Parma ham**

15ml/1 tbsp **olive oil**

120ml/4fl oz/½ cup **white wine**

salt and freshly ground **black pepper**

fresh **flat leaf parsley** sprigs, to garnish

cooked **tagliatelle** and sautéed **blewit mushrooms**, to serve (optional)

method

SERVES 4

1 Preheat the oven to 180ºC/350ºF/Gas 4. Melt about 10g/¼oz/ 2 tsp of the butter in a small pan and fry the garlic for a few seconds without browning. Spoon into a bowl.

2 Add the rice, ricotta, parsley and tarragon and season with salt and pepper. Stir to mix.

3 Place each chicken breast in turn between two sheets of clear film and flatten by beating lightly, but firmly, with a rolling pin.

4 Divide the slices of Parma ham between the chicken breasts, trimming the ham to fit, if necessary.

5 Place a spoonful of the rice stuffing at the wider end of each ham-topped breast. Roll up carefully and tie in place with cooking string or secure with a cocktail stick.

6 Heat the oil and the remaining butter in a frying pan and lightly fry the chicken rolls until browned on all sides. Place side by side in a shallow baking dish and pour over the white wine.

7 Cover the dish with greaseproof paper and cook in the oven for 30–35 minutes until the chicken is tender.

8 Cut the rolls into slices and serve on a bed of tagliatelle with sautéed blewit mushrooms and a generous grinding of black pepper, if you like. Garnish with sprigs of flat leaf parsley.

chicken liver risotto

THE **COMBINATION** OF CHICKEN LIVERS, BACON, PARSLEY AND THYME GIVES THIS RISOTTO A WONDERFULLY **RICH FLAVOUR**. SERVE IT AS A **STARTER** FOR FOUR OR A **LUNCH** FOR TWO OR THREE.

method

SERVES 2–4

1 Clean the chicken livers carefully, removing any fat or membrane. Rinse well, pat dry with kitchen paper and cut into small, even pieces.

2 Heat the oil and butter in a frying pan and fry the speck or bacon for 2–3 minutes.

3 Add the shallots, garlic and celery and continue frying for 3–4 minutes over a low heat until the vegetables are slightly softened. Increase the heat and add the chicken livers, stir-frying for a few minutes until they are brown all over.

4 Add the rice. Cook, stirring, for a few minutes, then pour over the wine. Allow to boil so that the alcohol is driven off. Stir frequently, taking care not to break up the chicken livers. When all the wine has been absorbed, add the hot stock, a ladleful at a time, stirring constantly.

5 About halfway through cooking, add the thyme and season with salt and pepper. Continue to add the stock as before, making sure that each quantity has been absorbed before adding more.

6 When the rice is tender but still has a bit of "bite", stir in the parsley. Taste and adjust the seasoning. Remove the pan from the heat, cover and leave to rest before serving, garnished with parsley and thyme.

ingredients

175g/6oz **chicken livers**
about 15ml/1 tbsp **olive oil**
about 25g/1oz/2 tbsp **butter**
about 40g/1½oz **speck** or
   3 rindless **streaky bacon**
   rashers, finely chopped
2 **shallots**, finely chopped
1 **garlic** clove, crushed
1 **celery** stick, finely sliced
275g/10oz/1½ cups **risotto rice**
175ml/6fl oz/¾ cup **dry white**
   wine
900ml–1 litre/1½–1¾ pints/
   3¾–4 cups simmering
   chicken stock
5ml/1 tsp chopped fresh **thyme**
15ml/1 tbsp chopped fresh **parsley**
salt and freshly ground **black**
   pepper
parsley and **thyme** sprigs to
   garnish

THIS MAKES AN **EXCELLENT** STARTER FOR SIX OR COULD BE SERVED FOR HALF THAT NUMBER AS A **SUPPER** DISH. SERVE WITH **MANGETOUTS** AND SAUTÉED **RED PEPPER** SLICES.

ingredients

2 **duck breasts**
30ml/2 tbsp **brandy**
30ml/2 tbsp **orange juice**
15ml/1 tbsp **olive oil** (optional)
1 **onion**, finely chopped
1 **garlic** clove, crushed
275g/10oz/1½ cups **risotto rice**
1–1.2 litres/1¾–2 pints/
    4–5 cups simmering **duck**,
    turkey or **chicken stock**
5ml/1 tsp chopped fresh **thyme**
5ml/1 tsp chopped fresh **mint**
10ml/2 tsp grated **orange rind**
40g/1½oz/½ cup freshly grated
    Parmesan cheese
salt and freshly ground **black**
    pepper
strips of thinly pared **orange**
    rind, to garnish

duck risotto

method

SERVES 2–4

1 Score the fatty side of the duck breasts and rub them with salt. Put them, fat side down, in a heavy frying pan and dry-fry over a medium heat for 6–8 minutes to render the fat. Transfer the breasts to a plate and then pull away and discard the fat. Cut the flesh into strips about 2cm/¾in wide.

2 Pour all but 15ml/1 tbsp of the rendered duck fat from the pan into a cup or jug, then reheat the fat in the pan. Fry the duck slices for 2–3 minutes over a medium high heat until evenly brown but not overcooked. Add the brandy, heat to simmering point and then ignite, either by tilting the pan or using a taper.

3 When the flames have died down, add the orange juice and season with salt and pepper. Remove from the heat and set aside.

4 In a saucepan, heat either 15ml/1 tbsp of the remaining duck fat or use olive oil. Fry the onion and garlic over a gentle heat until the onion is soft but not browned. Add the rice and cook, stirring all the time, until the grains are coated in oil and have become slightly translucent around the edges.

5 Add the stock, a ladleful at a time, waiting for each quantity of stock to be absorbed completely before adding the next. Just before adding the final ladleful of stock, stir in the duck, with the thyme and mint. Continue cooking until the risotto is creamy and the rice is tender but still has a bit of "bite".

6 Add the orange rind and Parmesan. Taste and adjust the seasoning, then remove from the heat, cover the pan and leave to stand for a few minutes. Serve on individual plates, garnished with the pared orange rind.

fish & shellfish

salmon risotto with cucumber & tarragon

THIS **SIMPLE** RISOTTO IS COOKED **ALL IN ONE** GO, AND IS THEREFORE SIMPLER THAN THE USUAL RISOTTO. IF YOU PREFER TO COOK THE **TRADITIONAL** WAY, ADD THE **SALMON** TWO-THIRDS OF THE WAY THROUGH COOKING.

method

SERVES 4

1 Heat the butter in a large saucepan and add the spring onions and cucumber. Cook for 2–3 minutes without letting the spring onions colour.

2 Stir in the rice, then pour in the stock and wine. Bring to the boil, then lower the heat and simmer, uncovered, for 10 minutes, stirring occasionally.

3 Stir in the diced salmon and season to taste with salt and freshly ground black pepper. Continue cooking for a further 5 minutes, stirring occasionally, then switch off the heat. Cover and leave to stand for 5 minutes.

4 Remove the lid, add the chopped tarragon and mix lightly. Spoon into a warmed bowl and serve.

variation
Carnaroli risotto rice would be excellent in this risotto, although if it is not available, Arborio can be used instead.

ingredients

25g/1oz/2 tbsp **butter**

small bunch of **spring onions**, white parts only, chopped

1/2 **cucumber**, peeled, seeded and chopped

350g/12oz/1¾ cups **risotto rice**

1.2 litres/2 pints/5 cups hot **chicken** or **fish stock**

150ml/¼ pint/⅔ cup **dry white wine**

450g/1lb **salmon fillet**, skinned and diced

45ml/3 tbsp chopped fresh **tarragon**

salt and freshly ground **black pepper**

MONKFISH IS A **VERSATILE**, FIRM-TEXTURED FISH WITH A SUPERB **FLAVOUR**, WHICH IS ACCENTUATED WITH **LEMON GRASS** IN THIS SOPHISTICATED, **TASTY** RISOTTO.

ingredients

seasoned flour

about 450g/1lb **monkfish**, cut into cubes

30ml/2 tbsp **olive oil**

40g/1½oz/3 tbsp **butter**

2 **shallots**, finely chopped

1 **lemon grass** stalk, finely chopped

275g/10oz/1½ cups **risotto rice**, preferably Carnaroli

175ml/6fl oz/¾ cup **dry white wine**

1 litre/1¾ pints/4 cups simmering **fish stock**

30ml/2 tbsp chopped fresh **parsley**

salt and **white pepper**

dressed **salad leaves**, to serve

monkfish risotto

method   SERVES 4

1 Spoon the seasoned flour over the monkfish cubes in a bowl. Toss the monkfish until coated.

2 Heat 15ml/1 tbsp of the oil with half the butter in a frying pan. Fry the monkfish cubes over a medium to high heat for 3–4 minutes until cooked, turning occasionally. Transfer to a plate and set aside.

3 Heat the remaining oil and butter in a saucepan and fry the shallots over a low heat for about 4 minutes until soft but not brown. Add the lemon grass and cook for 1–2 minutes more.

4 Tip in the rice. Cook for 2–3 minutes, stirring, until the rice is coated with oil and is slightly translucent. Gradually add the wine and the hot stock, stirring and waiting until each ladleful has been absorbed before adding the next.

5 When the rice is about three-quarters cooked, stir in the monkfish. Continue to cook the risotto, adding the remaining stock and stirring constantly until the grains of rice are tender, but still retain a bit of "bite". Season with salt and white pepper.

6 Remove the pan from the heat, stir in the parsley and cover with the lid. Leave the risotto to stand for a few minutes before serving with a garnish of dressed salad leaves.

cook's tip
Lemon grass adds a subtle flavour to this dish. Remove the tough outer skin and chop the inner flesh finely.

trout & parma ham risotto rolls

THIS MAKES A **DELICIOUS** AND **ELEGANT** MEAL. THE RISOTTO –
MADE WITH PORCINI MUSHROOMS AND PRAWNS – IS A **FINE MATCH**
FOR THE **ROBUST FLAVOUR** OF THE TROUT ROLLS.

ingredients

4 **trout** fillets, skinned

4 slices **Parma ham**

caper berries, to garnish

For the risotto

30ml/2 tbsp **olive oil**

8 large raw **prawns**, peeled and
   deveined

1 medium **onion**, chopped

225g/8oz/generous 1 cup **risotto
   rice**

about 105ml/7 tbsp **white wine**

about 750ml/1¼ pints/3 cups
   simmering **fish** or **chicken
   stock**

15g/½oz/2 tbsp dried **porcini** or
   chanterelle mushrooms,
   soaked for 10 minutes in warm
   water to cover

salt and freshly ground **black
   pepper**

method

SERVES 4

1 First make the risotto. Heat the oil in a heavy-based saucepan or
   deep frying pan and fry the prawns very briefly until flecked with pink.
   Lift out on a slotted spoon and transfer to a plate.

2 Add the chopped onion to the oil remaining in the pan and fry over a
   gentle heat for 3–4 minutes until soft. Add the rice and stir for 3–4
   minutes until the grains are evenly coated in oil. Add 75ml/5 tbsp of
   the wine and then the stock, a little at a time, stirring over a gentle
   heat and allowing the rice to absorb the liquid before adding more.

3 Drain the mushrooms, reserving the liquid, and cut the larger ones in
   half. Towards the end of cooking, stir the mushrooms into the risotto
   with 15ml/1 tbsp of the reserved mushroom liquid. If the rice is not
   yet al dente, add a little more stock or mushroom liquid and cook for
   2–3 minutes more. Season to taste with salt and pepper.

4 Remove the pan from the heat and stir in the prawns. Preheat the
   oven to 190°C/375°F/Gas 5.

5 Take a trout fillet, place a spoonful of risotto at one end and roll up.
   Wrap each fillet in a slice of Parma ham and place in a greased
   ovenproof dish.

6 Spoon any remaining risotto around the fish fillets and sprinkle over
   the rest of the wine. Cover loosely with foil and bake for 15–20
   minutes until the fish is tender. Spoon the risotto on to a platter, top
   with the trout rolls and garnish with caper berries. Serve at once.

cook's tip
There are no hard and fast rules about which type of risotto to use for this dish.
Almost any risotto recipe could be used, although a vegetable or seafood risotto
would be particularly suitable.

squid risotto with chilli & coriander

SQUID NEEDS TO BE COOKED EITHER VERY **QUICKLY** OR VERY **SLOWLY**. HERE THE SQUID IS **MARINATED** IN **LIME** AND **KIWI FRUIT** – A POPULAR METHOD IN NEW ZEALAND FOR TENDERIZING SQUID.

ingredients

about 450g/1lb **squid**

about 45ml/3 tbsp **olive oil**

15g/$\frac{1}{2}$oz/1 tbsp **butter**

1 **onion**, finely chopped

2 **garlic** cloves, crushed

1 fresh **red chilli**, seeded and finely sliced

275g/10oz/1$\frac{1}{2}$ cups **risotto rice**

175ml/6fl oz/$\frac{3}{4}$ cup **dry white wine**

1 litre/1$\frac{3}{4}$ pints/4 cups simmering **fish stock**

30ml/2 tbsp chopped fresh **coriander**

salt and freshly ground **black pepper**

For the marinade

2 ripe **kiwi fruit**, chopped and mashed

1 fresh **red chilli**, seeded and finely sliced

30ml/2 tbsp fresh **lime juice**

cook's tip
Although fish stock underlines the flavour of the squid, a light chicken or vegetable stock would also work well in this recipe.

method

SERVES 4

1 If not already cleaned, prepare the squid by cutting off the tentacles at the base and pulling to remove the quill. Discard the quill and intestines, if necessary, and pull away the thin outer skin. Rinse the body and cut into thin strips: cut the tentacles into short pieces, discarding the beak and eyes.

2 Mash the kiwi fruit for the marinade in a bowl, then stir in the chilli and lime juice. Add the squid, stirring to coat all the strips in the mixture. Season with salt and freshly ground black pepper, cover with clear film and set aside in the fridge for 4 hours or overnight.

3 Drain the squid. Heat 15ml/1 tbsp of the olive oil in a frying pan and cook the strips, in batches if necessary, for about 30–60 seconds over a high heat. It is important that the squid cooks very quickly. Transfer the cooked squid to a plate and set aside. Don't worry if some of the marinade clings to the squid, but if too much juice accumulates in the pan, pour this into a jug and add more olive oil when cooking the next batch, so that the squid fries rather than simmers. Reserve the accumulated juices in a jug.

4 Heat the remaining oil with the butter in a large saucepan and gently fry the onion and garlic for 5–6 minutes, until soft. Add the sliced chilli to the saucepan and fry for 1 minute more.

5 Add the rice. Cook for a few minutes, stirring, until the rice is coated with oil and is slightly translucent, then stir in the wine until it has been absorbed.

THIS IS A **FRESH-FLAVOURED** RISOTTO WHICH MAKES A WONDERFUL MAIN COURSE OR STARTER. YOU WILL NEED TWO **CRABS** FOR THIS RECIPE, AND IT IS THEREFORE A GOOD DISH TO FOLLOW A **VISIT TO THE SEASIDE**, WHERE CRABS ARE CHEAP AND PLENTIFUL.

ingredients

2 large cooked **crabs**
15ml/1 tbsp **olive oil**
25g/1oz/2 tbsp **butter**
2 **shallots**, finely chopped
275g/10oz/1½ cups **risotto rice**, preferably Carnaroli
75ml/5 tbsp **Marsala** or **brandy**
1 litre/1¾ pints/4 cups simmering **fish stock**
5ml/1 tsp chopped fresh **tarragon**
5ml/1 tsp chopped fresh **parsley**
60ml/4 tbsp **double cream**
salt and freshly ground **black pepper**

crab risotto

method   SERVES 4

1 First remove the crab meat from each of the shells in turn. Hold the crab firmly in one hand and hit the back underside firmly with the heel of your hand. This should loosen the shell from the body. Using your thumbs, push against the body and pull away from the shell. From the inside of the shell, remove and discard the intestines.

2 Discard the grey gills (dead man's fingers). Break off the claws and legs from the body, then use a small hammer or crackers to break them open. Using a pick, remove the meat from the claws and legs. Place the meat on a plate.

3 Using a pick or a skewer, pick out the white meat from the body cavities and place on the plate with the meat from the claws and legs, reserving some white meat to garnish. Scoop out the brown meat from inside the shell and set aside with the white meat on the plate.

4 Heat the oil and butter in a pan and gently fry the shallots until soft but not browned. Add the rice. Cook for a few minutes, stirring, until the rice is slightly translucent, then add the Marsala or brandy, bring to the boil, and cook, stirring, until the liquid has evaporated. Add a ladleful of hot stock and cook, stirring, until all the stock has been absorbed. Continue cooking in this way until about two-thirds of the stock has been added, then carefully stir in all the crab meat and the herbs.

5 Continue to cook the risotto, adding the remaining stock. When the rice is almost cooked but still has a slight "bite", remove it from the heat, stir in the cream and adjust the seasoning. Cover and leave to stand for 3 minutes to finish cooking. Serve garnished with the reserved white crab meat.

shellfish risotto with mixed mushrooms

THIS IS A **QUICK AND EASY** RISOTTO, WHERE ALL THE LIQUID IS ADDED IN **ONE GO**. THE METHOD IS WELL-SUITED TO THIS SHELLFISH DISH, AS IT MEANS EVERYTHING COOKS **TOGETHER** UNDISTURBED.

method

SERVES 4

1 Scrub the mussels and clams clean and discard any that are open and do not close when tapped with a knife. Set aside. Heat the oil in a large frying pan and fry the onion for 6–8 minutes until soft but not browned.

2 Add the rice, stirring to coat the grains in oil, then pour in the stock and wine and cook for 5 minutes. Add the mushrooms and cook for 5 minutes more, stirring occasionally.

3 Add the prawns, squid, mussels and clams and stir into the rice. Cover the pan and simmer over a low heat for 15 minutes until the prawns have turned pink and the mussels and clams have opened. Discard any of the shellfish that remain closed.

4 Switch off the heat. Add the truffle oil, if using, and stir in the herbs. Cover tightly and leave to stand for 5–10 minutes to allow all the flavours to blend. Season to taste with celery salt and a pinch of cayenne, pile into a warmed dish, and serve immediately.

ingredients

225g/8oz live **mussels**
225g/8oz live **Venus** or **carpet shell clams**
45ml/3 tbsp **olive oil**
1 **onion**, chopped
450g/1lb/2⅓ cups **risotto rice**
1.75 litres/3 pints/7½ cups simmering **chicken** or **vegetable stock**
150ml/¼ pint/⅔ cup **white wine**
225g/8oz/2–3 cups **assorted wild** and **cultivated mushrooms**, trimmed and sliced
115g/4oz raw peeled **prawns**, deveined
1 medium or 2 small **squid**, cleaned, trimmed and sliced
3 drops **truffle oil** (optional)
75ml/5 tbsp chopped **mixed fresh parsley** and **chervil**
celery salt and **cayenne pepper**

FRESH **ROOT GINGER** AND CORIANDER ADD A DISTINCTIVE **FLAVOUR** TO THIS DISH, WHILE THE GREEN CHILLIES GIVE IT A LITTLE **HEAT**. THE CHILLIES COULD BE OMITTED FOR A **MILDER** DISH.

ingredients

900g/2lb fresh **mussels**

about 250ml/8fl oz/1 cup **dry white wine**

30ml/2 tbsp **olive oil**

1 **onion**, chopped

2 **garlic** cloves, crushed

1–2 fresh **green chillies**, seeded and finely sliced

2.5cm/1in piece of fresh **root ginger**, grated

275g/10oz/1½ cups **risotto rice**

900ml/1½ pints/3¾ cups simmering **fish stock**

30ml/2 tbsp chopped fresh **coriander**

30ml/2 tbsp **double cream**

salt and freshly ground **black pepper**

mussel risotto

method

SERVES 4

1 Scrub the mussels, discarding any that do not close when sharply tapped. Place in a large saucepan. Add 120ml/4fl oz/½ cup of the wine and bring to the boil. Cover the pan and cook the mussels for 4–5 minutes until they have opened, shaking the pan occasionally. Drain, reserving the liquid and discarding any mussels that have not opened. Remove most of the mussels from their shells, reserving a few in their shells for decoration. Strain the mussel liquid.

2 Heat the oil and fry the onion and garlic for 3–4 minutes until beginning to soften. Add the chillies. Continue to cook over a low heat for 1–2 minutes, stirring frequently, then stir in the ginger and fry gently for 1 minute more.

3 Add the rice and cook over a medium heat for 2 minutes, stirring, until the rice is coated in oil and becomes translucent.

4 Stir in the reserved cooking liquid from the mussels. When this has been absorbed, add the remaining wine and cook, stirring until this has been absorbed. Now add the hot fish stock, a little at a time, making sure each addition has been absorbed before adding the next.

5 When the rice is about three-quarters cooked, stir in the mussels. Add the coriander and season with salt and pepper. Continue adding stock to the risotto until it is creamy and the rice is tender but slightly firm in the centre.

6 Remove the risotto from the heat, stir in the cream, cover and leave to rest for a few minutes. Spoon into a warmed serving dish, decorate with the reserved mussels in their shells, and serve immediately.

truffle & lobster risotto

TO CAPTURE THE **PRECIOUS QUALITIES** OF THE FRESH TRUFFLE, PARTNER IT WITH **LOBSTER** AND SERVE IN A **SILKY SMOOTH** RISOTTO. BOTH TRUFFLE SHAVINGS AND TRUFFLE OIL ARE ADDED TOWARDS THE END OF COOKING TO PRESERVE THEIR **FLAVOUR**.

method

SERVES 4

1 Melt the butter, add the onion and fry until soft. Add the rice and stir well to coat with fat.

2 Add the thyme, then the wine, and cook until it has been absorbed. Add the chicken stock a little at a time, stirring. Let each ladleful be absorbed before adding the next.

3 Twist off the lobster tail, cut the underside with scissors and remove the white tail meat. Carefully break open the claws with a small kitchen hammer and remove the flesh. Cut half the meat into big chunks, then roughly chop the remainder.

4 Stir in the chopped lobster meat, half the chopped herbs and the truffle oil. Season to taste. Remove the rice from the heat, cover and leave to stand for 5 minutes.

5 Divide among warmed plates and centre the lobster chunks on top. Cut the hard-boiled eggs into wedges and arrange them around the lobster meat. Finally, shave fresh truffle over each portion and sprinkle with the remaining herbs. Serve immediately.

ingredients

50g/2oz/4 tbsp unsalted **butter**

1 medium **onion**, chopped

350g/12oz/1¾ cups **risotto rice**, preferably Carnaroli

1 fresh **thyme** sprig

150ml/¼ pint/⅔ cup **dry white wine**

1.2 litres/2 pints/5 cups simmering **chicken stock**

1 freshly cooked **lobster**

45ml/3 tbsp chopped mixed fresh **parsley** and **chervil**

3–4 drops **truffle oil**

2 hard-boiled **eggs**

1 fresh black or white **truffle**

salt and freshly ground **black pepper**

cook's tip

To make the most of the aromatic truffle scent, keep the tuber in the rice jar for a few days before use.

scallop risotto

TRY TO BUY **FRESH SCALLOPS** FOR THIS DISH. THEY COME WITH THE **CORAL** ATTACHED, WHICH ADDS **FLAVOUR**, **TEXTURE** AND **COLOUR**.

method

SERVES 4

1 Separate the scallops from their corals. Cut the white flesh in half or into 2cm/¾in slices.

2 Melt half the butter with 5ml/1 tsp oil. Fry the white parts of the scallops for 2–3 minutes. Pour over the Pernod, heat for a few seconds, then ignite and allow to flame for a few seconds. When the flames have died down, remove the pan from the heat.

3 Heat the remaining butter and olive oil in a pan and fry the shallots for about 3–4 minutes, until soft but not browned. Add the rice and cook for a few minutes, stirring, until the rice is coated with oil and is beginning to turn translucent around the edges.

4 Gradually add the hot stock, a ladleful at a time, stirring constantly and waiting for each ladleful of stock to be absorbed before adding the next.

5 When the rice is very nearly cooked, add the scallops and all the juices from the pan, together with the corals, the saffron milk, parsley and seasoning. Stir well to mix. Continue cooking, adding the remaining stock and stirring occasionally, until the risotto is thick and creamy.

6 Remove the pan from the heat, stir in the double cream and cover. Leave the risotto to rest for about 3 minutes to complete the cooking, then pile it into a warmed bowl and serve.

ingredients

about 12 **scallops**, with their corals
50g/2oz/4 tbsp **butter**
15ml/1 tbsp **olive oil**
30ml/2 tbsp **Pernod**
2 **shallots**, finely chopped
275g/10oz/1½ cups **risotto rice**
1 litre/1¾ pints/4 cups simmering **fish stock**
generous pinch of **saffron** strands, dissolved in 15ml/1 tbsp warm **milk**
30ml/2 tbsp chopped fresh **parsley**
60ml/4 tbsp **double cream**
salt and freshly ground **black pepper**

YOU CAN USE **ANY SEAFOOD** FOR THIS RISOTTO, AS LONG AS THE TOTAL WEIGHT IS THE SAME.

ingredients

450g/1lb fresh **mussels**

250ml/8fl oz/1 cup **dry white wine**

225g/8oz **sea bass fillet**, skinned and cut into pieces

seasoned flour

60ml/4 tbsp **olive oil**

8 **scallops** with corals separated, white parts halved or sliced, if large

225g/8oz **squid**, cleaned, cut into rings

12 large raw **prawns**

2 **shallots**, finely chopped

1 **garlic** clove, crushed

400g/14oz/2 cups **risotto rice**,

3 **tomatoes**, peeled, seeded and chopped

1.5 litres/2½ pints/6¼ cups simmering **fish stock**

30ml/2 tbsp chopped fresh **parsley**

30ml/2 tbsp **double cream**

salt and ground **black pepper**

seafood risotto

method

SERVES 4

1 Scrub the mussels, discarding any that do not close when sharply tapped. Place them in a large saucepan and add 90ml/6 tbsp of the wine. Bring to the boil, cover the pan and cook for 3–4 minutes until all the mussels have opened, shaking the pan occasionally. Drain, reserving the liquid and discarding any mussels that have not opened. Set aside a few mussels in their shells for garnishing; remove the others from their shells. Strain the cooking liquid.

2 Dust the pieces of sea bass in seasoned flour. Heat 30ml/2 tbsp of the olive oil in a frying pan and fry the fish for 3–4 minutes until cooked. Transfer to a plate. Add a little more oil to the pan and fry the white parts of the scallops for 1–2 minutes on both sides until tender. Transfer to a plate. Fry the squid for 3–4 minutes in the same pan, adding a little more oil if necessary, then set aside. Lastly, add the prawns and fry for a further 3–4 minutes until pink, turning frequently.

3 Towards the end of cooking, add a splash of wine – about 30ml/2 tbsp – and continue cooking so that the prawns become tender, but do not burn. Remove the prawns from the pan. As soon as they are cool enough to handle, remove the shells and legs, leaving the tails intact.

4 In a large saucepan, heat the remaining olive oil and fry the shallots and garlic for 3–4 minutes over a gentle heat until the shallots are soft but not brown. Add the rice and cook for a few minutes, stirring, until the rice is coated with oil and the grains are slightly translucent. Stir in the tomatoes, with the reserved liquid from the mussels. When all the free liquid has been absorbed, add the remaining wine, stirring constantly. When it has also been absorbed, gradually add the hot stock, one ladleful at a time, continuing to stir the rice constantly and waiting until each quantity of stock has been absorbed before adding the next.

5 When the risotto is three-quarters cooked, carefully stir in all the seafood, except the mussels reserved for the garnish. Continue to cook until all the stock has been absorbed and the rice is tender but still has a bit of "bite". Stir in the parsley and cream and adjust the seasoning. Cover the pan and leave the risotto to stand for 2–3 minutes. Serve in individual bowls, garnished with the reserved mussels in their shells.

beyond risotto

ONE OF THE **GLORIOUS** THINGS ABOUT FOOD FROM THE SOUTH OF **FRANCE** IS ITS BRIGHT **COLOUR**.

ingredients

2 **onions**

90ml/6 tbsp **olive oil**

175g/6oz/scant 1 cup **brown long grain rice**

10ml/2 tsp **mustard seeds**

475ml/16fl oz/2 cups **vegetable stock**

1 large or 2 small **red peppers**, seeded and cut into chunks

1 small **aubergine**, cut into cubes

2–3 **courgettes**, sliced

about 12 **cherry tomatoes**

5–6 fresh **basil** leaves, torn into pieces

2 **garlic** cloves, finely chopped

60ml/4 tbsp **white wine**

60ml/4 tbsp **passata**

2 hard-boiled **eggs**, cut into wedges

8 stuffed **green olives**, sliced

15ml/1 tbsp **capers**

3 drained **sun-dried tomatoes** in **oil**, sliced (optional)

butter

sea salt and freshly ground **black pepper**

provençal rice

method

SERVES 4

1 Preheat the oven to 200°C/400°F/Gas 6. Finely chop one onion. Heat 30ml/2 tbsp of the oil in a saucepan and fry the chopped onion over a gentle heat for 5–6 minutes until softened.

2 Add the rice and mustard seeds. Cook, stirring, for 2 minutes, then add the stock and a little salt. Bring to the boil, then lower the heat, cover and simmer for 35 minutes until the rice is tender.

3 Meanwhile, cut the remaining onion into wedges. Put these in a roasting tin with the peppers, aubergine, courgettes and cherry tomatoes. Scatter over the torn basil leaves and chopped garlic. Pour over the remaining olive oil and sprinkle with sea salt and black pepper. Roast for 15–20 minutes until the vegetables begin to char, stirring halfway through cooking. Reduce the oven temperature to 180°C/350°F/Gas 4.

4 Spoon the rice into an earthenware casserole. Put the roasted vegetables on top, together with any vegetable juices from the roasting tin, then pour over the wine and passata.

5 Arrange the egg wedges on top of the vegetables, with the sliced olives, capers and sun-dried tomatoes, if using. Dot with butter, cover and cook for 15–20 minutes until heated through.

chicken biryani

AN IDEAL **INDIAN** DISH FOR A **SPECIAL SUPPER**.

method

SERVES 4

1 Preheat the oven to 190°C/375°F/Gas 5. Remove the seeds from half the cardamom pods and grind them finely, using a pestle and mortar. Set them aside. Bring a pan of water to the boil and add the rice, salt, whole cardamom pods, cloves and cinnamon stick. Boil for 2 minutes, then drain, leaving the whole spices in the rice.

2 Heat the oil in a frying pan and fry the onions for 8 minutes, until softened and browned. Add the chicken and the ground spices, including the ground cardamom seeds. Mix well, then add the garlic, ginger and lemon juice. Stir-fry for 5 minutes.

3 Transfer the chicken mixture to a casserole and arrange the tomatoes on top. Sprinkle on the fresh coriander, spoon the yogurt evenly on top and cover with the drained rice.

4 Drizzle the saffron milk over the rice and pour over the water. Cover tightly and bake for 1 hour. Transfer to a warmed serving platter and remove the whole spices from the rice. Garnish with toasted almonds and fresh coriander sprigs and serve with the natural yogurt.

ingredients

10 whole green **cardamom pods**
275g/10oz/1½ cups **basmati rice**, soaked and drained
2.5ml/½ tsp **salt**
2–3 whole **cloves**
5cm/2in **cinnamon stick**
45ml/3 tbsp **vegetable oil**
3 **onions**, sliced
4 **chicken breasts**, each about 175g/6oz, cubed
1.5ml/¼ tsp ground **cloves**
1.5ml/¼ tsp hot **chilli powder**
5ml/1 tsp ground **cumin**
5ml/1 tsp ground **coriander**
2.5ml/½ tsp ground **black pepper**
3 **garlic** cloves, chopped
5ml/1 tsp finely chopped fresh **root ginger**
juice of 1 **lemon**
4 **tomatoes**, sliced
30ml/2 tbsp chopped fresh **coriander**
150ml/¼ pint/⅔ cup **natural yogurt**
4–5 **saffron strands**, soaked in 10ml/2 tsp hot **milk**
150ml/¼ pint/⅔ cup **water**
toasted flaked **almonds** and fresh **coriander** sprigs, to garnish
natural yogurt, to serve

chicken & basil coconut rice

FOR THIS DISH, THE RICE IS **PARTIALLY BOILED** BEFORE BEING SIMMERED WITH **COCONUT** SO THAT IT FULLY ABSORBS THE FLAVOUR OF THE **CHILLIES**, **BASIL** AND **SPICES**.

ingredients

350g/12oz/1¾ cups **Thai fragrant rice**, rinsed

30–45ml/2–3 tbsp **groundnut oil**

1 large **onion**, finely sliced into rings

1 **garlic** clove, crushed

1 fresh **red chilli**, seeded and finely sliced

1 fresh **green chilli**, seeded and finely sliced

generous handful of **basil leaves**

3 skinless, boneless **chicken breasts**, about 350g/12oz, finely sliced

5mm/¼in piece of **lemon grass**, pounded or finely chopped

50g/2oz piece of **creamed coconut** dissolved in 600ml/ 1 pint/2½ cups boiling **water**

salt and freshly ground **black pepper**

method

SERVES 4

1 Bring a saucepan of lightly salted water to the boil. Add the rice to the pan and boil for about 6 minutes, until partially cooked. Drain.

2 Heat the oil in a frying pan and fry the onion rings for 5–10 minutes until golden and crisp. Lift out, drain on kitchen paper and set aside.

3 Fry the garlic and chillies in the oil remaining in the pan for 2–3 minutes, then add the basil leaves and fry briefly until they begin to wilt. Remove a few leaves and set them aside for the garnish, then add the chicken slices with the lemon grass and fry for 2–3 minutes until golden.

4 Add the rice. Stir-fry for a few minutes to coat the grains, then pour in the coconut liquid. Cook for 4–5 minutes or until the rice is tender, adding a little more water if necessary. Adjust the seasoning. Pile the rice into a warmed serving dish, scatter with the fried onion rings and basil leaves, and serve immediately.

indonesian pineapple rice

THIS WAY OF PRESENTING RICE NOT ONLY LOOKS **SPECTACULAR**, IT ALSO TASTES SO **GOOD** THAT IT CAN EASILY BE **SERVED SOLO**.

ingredients

75g/3oz/¾ cup natural **peanuts**

1 large **pineapple**

45ml/3 tbsp **groundnut** or **sunflower oil**

1 **onion**, chopped

1 **garlic** clove, crushed

2 **chicken breasts**, about 225g/8oz, cut into strips

225g/8oz/generous 1 cup **Thai fragrant rice**, rinsed

600ml/1 pint/2½ cups **chicken stock**

1 **lemon grass** stalk, bruised

2 thick slices of **ham**, cut into julienne strips

1 fresh **red chilli**, seeded and very finely sliced

salt

method

SERVES 4

1 Dry-fry the peanuts in a non-stick frying pan until golden. When cool, grind one-sixth of them in a coffee or herb mill and chop the remainder.

2 Cut a lengthways slice of pineapple, slicing through the leaves, then cut out the flesh to leave a neat shell. Chop 115g/4oz of the pineapple into cubes; saving the remainder for another dish.

3 Heat the oil in a saucepan and fry the onion and garlic for 3–4 minutes until soft. Add the chicken strips and stir-fry over a medium heat for a few minutes until evenly brown.

4 Add the rice to the pan. Toss with the chicken mixture for a few minutes, then pour in the stock, with the lemon grass and a little salt. Bring to just below boiling point, then lower the heat, cover the pan and simmer gently for 10–12 minutes until both the rice and the chicken pieces are tender.

5 Stir the chopped peanuts, the pineapple cubes and the ham into the rice, then spoon the mixture into the pineapple shell. Sprinkle the ground peanuts and the sliced chilli over the top and serve.

peruvian duck with rice

THIS IS A VERY **RICH** DISH, BRIGHTLY **COLOURED** WITH **SPANISH TOMATOES** AND **FRESH HERBS**.

ingredients

- 4 boned **duck breasts**
- 1 **Spanish onion,** chopped
- 2 **garlic** cloves, crushed
- 10ml/2 tsp grated fresh **root ginger**
- 4 **tomatoes** (peeled, if liked), chopped
- 225g/8oz **Kabocha** or **onion squash,** cut into 1cm/1/2in cubes
- 275g/10oz/1 1/2 cups **long grain rice**
- 750ml/1 1/4 pints/3 cups **chicken stock**
- 15ml/1 tbsp finely chopped fresh **coriander**
- 15ml/1 tbsp finely chopped fresh **mint**
- **salt** and freshly ground **black pepper**

method

SERVES 4

1 Heat a heavy-based frying pan or flameproof casserole. Using a sharp knife, score the fatty side of the duck breasts in a criss-cross pattern, rub the fat with a little salt, then dry-fry the duck, skin side down, for 6–8 minutes to render some of the fat.

2 Pour all but 15ml/1 tbsp of the fat into a jar or cup, then fry the breasts, meat side down, in the fat remaining in the pan for 3–4 minutes until brown all over. Transfer to a board, slice thickly and set aside in a shallow dish. Deglaze the pan with a little water and pour this liquid over the duck.

3 Fry the onion and garlic in the same pan for 4–5 minutes until the onion is fairly soft, adding a little extra duck fat if necessary. Stir in the ginger, cook for 1–2 minutes more, then add the tomatoes and cook, stirring, for another 2 minutes.

4 Add the squash, stir-fry for a few minutes, then cover and allow to steam for about 4 minutes.

5 Stir in the rice and cook, stirring, until the rice is coated in the tomato and onion mixture. Pour in the stock, return the slices of duck to the pan and season with salt and pepper.

6 Bring to the boil, then lower the heat, cover and simmer gently for 30–35 minutes until the rice is tender. Stir in the coriander and mint and serve.

---

cook's tip
While rice was originally imported to South America, squash was very much an indigenous vegetable. Pumpkin could also be used for this recipe. Kabocha squash has a thick skin and lots of seeds, which need to be removed before the flesh is cubed.

THIS **INDIAN** DISH IS SIMILAR TO **BIRYANI**, BUT HERE THE LAMB IS MARINATED WITH THE **YOGURT**. SERVE WITH A **DHAL** OR SPICED **MUSHROOMS**.

ingredients

900g/2lb **lamb fillet**, cut into 2.5cm/1in cubes

60ml/4 tbsp **ghee** or **butter**

2 **onions**, sliced

450g/1lb **potatoes**, cut into large chunks

chicken stock or **water**

450g/1lb/2⅓ cups **basmati rice**, soaked

generous pinch of **saffron strands**, dissolved in 30ml/ 2 tbsp **warm milk**

fresh **coriander** sprigs, to garnish

For the marinade

475ml/16fl oz/2 cups **natural yogurt**

3–4 **garlic** cloves, crushed

10ml/2 tsp **cayenne pepper**

20ml/4 tsp **garam masala**

10ml/2 tsp ground **cumin**

5ml/1 tsp ground **coriander**

lamb parsi

method

SERVES 4

1 Make the marinade by mixing all the ingredients in a large bowl. Add the meat, stir to coat, then cover and leave to marinate for 3–4 hours in a cool place or overnight in the fridge.

2 Melt 30ml/2 tbsp of the ghee or butter in a large saucepan and fry the onions for 6–8 minutes until lightly golden. Transfer to a plate.

3 Melt a further 25ml/1½ tbsp of the ghee or butter in the pan. Fry the marinated lamb cubes in batches until evenly brown, transferring each batch in turn to a plate. When all the lamb has been browned, return it to the pan and scrape in the remaining marinade.

4 Stir in the potatoes and add about three-quarters of the fried onions. Pour in just enough chicken stock or water to cover the mixture. Bring to the boil, then cover and simmer over a very low heat for 40–50 minutes until the lamb is tender and the potatoes are cooked. Preheat the oven to 160°C/325°F/Gas 3.

5 Drain the rice. Cook it in a pan of boiling stock or water for 5 minutes. Meanwhile, spoon the lamb mixture into a casserole. Drain the rice and mound it on top of the lamb, then, using the handle of a wooden spoon, make a hole down the centre. Top with the remaining fried onions, pour the saffron milk over the top and dot with the remaining ghee or butter.

6 Cover the pan with a double layer of foil and a lid. Cook in the oven for 30–35 minutes or until the rice is completely tender. Garnish with fresh coriander sprigs and serve.

african lamb & vegetable pilau

SPICY LAMB IS SERVED IN THIS DISH WITH BASMATI RICE AND A COLOURFUL **SELECTION** OF DIFFERENT **VEGETABLES** AND **CASHEW** NUTS. LAMB AND RICE ARE **POPULAR** IN **AFRICA**.

method

SERVES 4

1 Put the lamb cubes in a large bowl and add the thyme, paprika, garam masala and garlic, with plenty of salt and pepper. Stir, cover, and leave in a cool place for 2–3 hours.

2 Heat the oil in a saucepan and fry the lamb, in batches if necessary, over a medium heat for 5–6 minutes, until browned. Stir in the stock, cover the pan and cook for 35–40 minutes. Using a slotted spoon, transfer the lamb to a bowl. Pour the liquid into a measuring jug, topping it up with water if necessary to make 600ml/1 pint/2½ cups.

3 Melt the butter in a separate pan and fry the onion, potato and carrot for 5 minutes. Add the red pepper and chilli and fry for 3 minutes more, then stir in the cabbage, yogurt, spices, garlic and the reserved lamb stock. Stir well, cover, then simmer gently for 5–10 minutes, until the cabbage has wilted.

4 Drain the rice and stir into the stew with the lamb. Cover and simmer over a low heat for 20 minutes or until the rice is cooked. Sprinkle in the cashew nuts and season to taste with salt and pepper. Serve hot, cupped in cabbage or lettuce leaves.

ingredients

450g/1lb boned shoulder of **lamb**, cubed

2.5ml/½ tsp dried **thyme**

2.5ml/½ tsp **paprika**

5ml/1 tsp **garam masala**

1 **garlic** clove, crushed

25ml/1½ tbsp **vegetable oil**

900ml/1½ pints/3¾ cups **lamb stock**

savoy cabbage or crisp **lettuce leaves**, to serve

For the rice

25g/1oz/2 tbsp **butter**

1 **onion**, chopped

1 medium **potato**, diced

1 **carrot**, sliced

½ **red pepper**, seeded & chopped

1 fresh **green chilli**, seeded & chopped

115g/4oz/1 cup sliced green **cabbage**

60ml/4 tbsp **natural yogurt**

2.5ml/½ tsp ground **cumin**

5 green **cardamom pods**

2 **garlic** cloves, crushed

225g/8oz/generous 1 cup **basmati rice**, soaked

50g/2oz/½ cup **cashew nuts**

salt and ground **black pepper**

louisiana rice

AUBERGINE AND **PORK** COMBINE WITH HERBS AND SPICES TO MAKE A HIGHLY **FLAVOURSOME** DISH.

method

SERVES 4

1 Heat the oil in a frying pan. When it is piping hot, add the onion and aubergine and stir-fry for about 5 minutes.

2 Add the pork and cook for 6–8 minutes until browned, using a wooden spoon to break up any lumps.

3 Stir in the green pepper, celery and garlic, with all the spices and herbs. Cover and cook over a high heat for 9–10 minutes, stirring frequently from the bottom of the pan to scrape up and distribute the crispy brown bits.

4 Pour in the chicken stock and stir to remove any sediment from the bottom of the pan. Cover and cook for 6 minutes over a moderate heat. Stir in the chicken livers and cook for 2 minutes more.

5 Stir in the rice and add the bay leaf. Lower the heat, cover and simmer for 6–7 minutes. Turn off the heat and leave to stand, still covered, for 10–15 minutes more until the rice is tender. Remove the bay leaf and stir in the chopped parsley. Serve the rice hot.

ingredients

60ml/4 tbsp **vegetable oil**

1 **onion,** chopped

1 small **aubergine,** diced

225g/8oz minced **pork**

1 **green pepper,** seeded and chopped

2 **celery** sticks, chopped

1 **garlic** clove, crushed

5ml/1 tsp **cayenne pepper**

5ml/1 tsp **paprika**

5ml/1 tsp freshly ground **black pepper**

2.5ml/½ tsp **salt**

5ml/1 tsp dried **thyme**

2.5ml/½ tsp dried **oregano**

475ml/16fl oz/2 cups **chicken stock**

225g/8oz **chicken livers,** chopped

150g/5oz/¾ cup **white long grain rice**

1 **bay leaf**

45ml/3 tbsp chopped fresh **parsley**

ingredients

2 large skinless, boneless **chicken breasts**

about 150g/5oz prepared **squid,** cut into rings

275g/10oz **cod** or **haddock** fillets, skinned and cut into bite-size chunks

8–10 raw **king prawns,** peeled and deveined

8 **scallops,** trimmed and halved

350g/12oz fresh **mussels**

250g/9oz/1⅓ cups **white long grain rice**

30ml/2 tbsp **sunflower oil**

1 bunch **spring onions**, cut into strips

2 small **courgettes,** cut into strips

1 **red pepper,** cored, seeded and cut into strips

400ml/14fl oz/1⅔ cups **chicken stock**

250ml/8fl oz/1 cup **passata**

salt and freshly ground **black pepper**

fresh **coriander** sprigs and **lemon** wedges, to garnish

For the marinade

2 fresh **red chillies,** seeded and roughly chopped

generous handful of fresh **coriander**

10–15ml/2–3 tsp ground **cumin**

15ml/1 tbsp **paprika**

2 **garlic** cloves

45ml/3 tbsp **olive oil**

60ml/4 tbsp **sunflower oil**

juice of 1 **lemon**

moroccan paella

method

SERVES 6

1 Make the marinade. Place all the ingredients in a food processor with 5ml/1 tsp salt and process until thoroughly blended. Cut the chicken into bite-size pieces. Place in a bowl.

2 Place the fish and shellfish (apart from the mussels) in a separate glass bowl. Divide the marinade between the fish and chicken and stir well. Cover with clear film and leave to marinate for at least 2 hours.

3 Scrub the mussels, discarding any that do not close when tapped sharply, and keep in a bowl in the fridge until ready to use. Place the rice in a bowl, cover with boiling water and set aside for about 30 minutes. Drain the chicken and fish, and reserve both lots of the marinade. Heat the oil in a wok, balti pan or paella pan and fry the chicken pieces for a few minutes until lightly browned.

4 Add the spring onions to the pan, fry for 1 minute and then add the courgettes and red pepper and fry for 3–4 minutes more until slightly softened. Transfer the chicken and then the vegetables to separate plates.

5 Scrape all the marinade into the pan and cook for 1 minute. Drain the rice, add to the pan and cook for 1 minute. Add the chicken stock, passata and reserved chicken, season with salt and pepper and stir well. Bring the mixture to the boil, then cover the pan with a large lid or foil and simmer very gently for 10–15 minutes until the rice is almost tender.

6 Add the reserved vegetables to the pan and place all the fish and mussels on top. Cover again with a lid or foil and cook over a moderate heat for 10–12 minutes until the fish is cooked and the mussels have opened. Discard any mussels that remain closed. Serve garnished with fresh coriander and lemon wedges.

persian rice with a tahdeeg

PERSIAN OR IRANIAN CUISINE IS **EXOTIC** AND **DELICIOUS**, AND THE FLAVOURS ARE **INTENSE**. A TAHDEEG IS THE GLORIOUS, **GOLDEN RICE** CRUST OR "DIG" THAT FORMS ON THE BOTTOM OF THE SAUCEPAN AS THE **RICE** COOKS.

ingredients

450g/1lb/2⅓ cups **basmati rice,** soaked
150ml/¼ pint/⅔ cup **sunflower oil**
2 **garlic** cloves, crushed
2 **onions,** 1 chopped, 1 finely sliced
150g/5oz/⅔ cup **green lentils,** soaked
600ml/1 pint/2½ cups **stock**
50g/2oz/⅓ cup **raisins**
10ml/2 tsp ground **coriander**
45ml/3 tbsp **tomato purée**
a few **saffron strands**
1 **egg yolk,** beaten
10ml/2 tsp **natural yogurt**
75g/3oz/6 tbsp melted **ghee** or **clarified butter**
salt and freshly ground **black pepper**

cook's tip
In Iran, aromatic white basmati rice would traditionally be used for this dish, but you could use any long grain rice, or a brown rice, if you prefer.

method

SERVES 4

1 Drain the rice, then cook it in plenty of boiling salted water for 3 minutes. Drain again.

2 Heat 30ml/2 tbsp of the oil in a large saucepan and fry the garlic and the chopped onion for 5 minutes. Stir in the lentils, stock, raisins, ground coriander and tomato purée, with salt and pepper to taste. Bring to the boil, then lower the heat, cover and simmer for about 20 minutes.

3 Soak the saffron strands in a little hot water. Mix the egg yolk and yogurt in a bowl. Spoon in about 120ml/4 fl oz/½ cup of the cooked rice and mix thoroughly. Season well.

4 Heat about two-thirds of the remaining oil in a large saucepan. Scatter the egg and yogurt rice evenly over the bottom of the pan.

5 Scatter the remaining rice into the pan, alternating it with the lentil mixture. Build up in a pyramid shape away from the sides of the pan, finishing with a layer of plain rice. With a long wooden spoon handle, make three holes down to the bottom of the pan; drizzle over the melted ghee or butter. Bring to a high heat, then wrap the pan lid in a clean, wet dish towel and place firmly on top. When a good head of steam appears, turn the heat down to low. Cook slowly for about 30 minutes.

6 Meanwhile, fry the onion slices in the remaining oil until browned and crisp. Drain well. Remove the rice pan from the heat, keeping it covered, and plunge the base briefly into a sink of cold water to loosen the rice on the bottom. Strain the saffron water into a bowl and stir in a few spoons of the white rice.

7 Toss the rice and lentils together in the pan and spoon out on to a serving dish, mounding the mixture. Scatter the saffron rice on top. Break up the rice crust on the bottom of the pan and place pieces of it around the mound. Scatter over the crispy fried onions and serve.

mushroom pilau

THIS DISH IS **SIMPLICITY** ITSELF. SERVE WITH ANY **INDIAN** DISH OR WITH **ROAST LAMB** OR **CHICKEN**.

method

SERVES 4

1 Heat the oil in a flameproof casserole and fry the shallots, garlic and cardamom pods over a medium heat for 3–4 minutes until the shallots have softened and are beginning to brown.

2 Add the ghee or butter. When it has melted, add the mushrooms and fry for 2–3 minutes more.

3 Add the rice, ginger and garam masala. Stir-fry over a low heat for 2–3 minutes, then stir in the water and a little salt. Bring to the boil, then cover tightly and simmer over a very low heat for 10 minutes.

4 Remove the casserole from the heat. Leave to stand, covered, for 5 minutes. Add the chopped coriander and fork it through the rice. Spoon into a serving bowl and serve at once.

ingredients

30ml/2 tbsp **vegetable oil**

2 **shallots**, finely chopped

1 **garlic** clove, crushed

3 **green cardamom pods**

25g/1oz/2 tbsp **ghee** or **butter**

175g/6oz/2½ cups **button mushrooms**, sliced

225g/8oz/generous 1 cup **basmati rice**, soaked

5ml/1 tsp grated fresh **root ginger**

good pinch of **garam masala**

450ml/¾ pint/scant 2 cups **water**

15ml/1 tbsp chopped fresh **coriander**

salt

THIS **TASTY** RICE DISH CAN BE SERVED WITH A **MEAT CURRY** OR AS PART OF A **VEGETARIAN** MEAL.

ingredients

30ml/2 tbsp **sunflower oil**

15ml/1 tbsp **ghee** or **butter**

1 **onion**, chopped

2 **garlic** cloves, crushed

3 **tomatoes**, peeled, seeded and chopped

225g/8oz/generous 1 cup **brown basmati rice**, soaked

10ml/2 tsp **dhana jeera powder** or 5ml/1 tsp ground **coriander** and 5ml/1 tsp ground **cumin**

2 **carrots**, coarsely grated

900ml/1½ pints/3¾ cups **vegetable stock**

275g/10oz baby **spinach** leaves, washed

50g/2oz/½ cup **unsalted cashew nuts**, toasted

salt and freshly ground **black pepper**

indian rice with tomatoes & spinach

method
SERVES 4

1 Heat the oil and ghee or butter in a flameproof casserole and gently fry the onion and garlic for 4–5 minutes until soft. Add the chopped tomatoes and cook for 3–4 minutes, stirring, until slightly thickened.

2 Drain the rice, add it to the casserole and cook gently for 1–2 minutes, stirring, until the rice is coated with the tomato and onion mixture.

3 Stir in the dhana jeera powder or coriander and cumin, then add the carrots and season with salt and pepper. Pour in the stock and stir well to mix.

4 Bring to the boil, then cover tightly and simmer over a very gentle heat for 20–25 minutes until the rice is tender. Lay the spinach on the surface of the rice, cover again and cook for 2–3 minutes until the spinach has wilted. Fold the spinach into the rest of the rice and check the seasoning. Sprinkle with cashews and serve.

cook's tip
If you can't get baby spinach leaves, use larger fresh spinach leaves. Remove any tough stalks and chop the leaves roughly.

VEGETARIANS WILL LOVE THIS SIMPLE **PILAU**. ADD WILD OR CULTIVATED **MUSHROOMS**, IF YOU LIKE.

ingredients

15–30ml/1–2 tbsp **sunflower oil**

1 **onion,** chopped

1 **garlic** clove, crushed

1 large **carrot,** coarsely grated

225g/8oz/generous 1 cup
    basmati rice, soaked

5ml/1 tsp **cumin** seeds

10ml/2 tsp ground **coriander**

10ml/2 tsp **black mustard
    seeds** (optional)

4 **green cardamom pods**

450ml/¾ pint/scant 2 cups
    vegetable stock or **water**

1 **bay leaf**

75g/3oz/¾ cup **unsalted
    walnuts** and **cashew nuts**

salt and freshly ground **black
    pepper**

fresh **parsley** or **coriander**
    sprigs, to garnish

basmati & nut pilau

method

SERVES 4

1 Heat the oil in a large, shallow frying pan and gently fry the onion, garlic and carrot for 3–4 minutes. Drain the rice and then add to the pan with the spices. Cook for 1–2 minutes more, stirring to coat the grains in oil.

2 Pour in the stock or water, add the bay leaf and season well. Bring to the boil, lower the heat, cover and simmer very gently for 10–12 minutes.

3 Remove the pan from the heat without lifting the lid. Leave to stand for about 5 minutes, then check the rice. If it is cooked, there will be small steam holes on the surface of the rice. Remove and discard the bay leaf and the cardamom pods.

4 Stir in the nuts and check the seasoning. Spoon on to a platter, garnish with the parsley or coriander and serve.

cook's tip
Use whichever nuts you prefer in this dish – even unsalted peanuts taste good, although almonds, cashew nuts or pistachios are more exotic.

chinese fried rice

THIS DISH, A VARIATION ON **SPECIAL FRIED RICE**, IS MORE **ELABORATE** THAN THE MORE FAMILIAR EGG FRIED RICE, AND IS ALMOST A **MEAL IN ITSELF**.

method

SERVES 4

1 Dice the cooked ham finely. Pat the cooked prawns dry on kitchen paper.

2 In a bowl, beat the eggs lightly with a pinch of the salt and a few pieces of the spring onions.

3 Heat about half the oil in a wok, stir-fry the peas, prawns and ham for 1 minute, then add the soy sauce and rice wine or sherry. Transfer to a bowl and keep hot.

4 Heat the remaining oil in the wok and scramble the eggs lightly. Add the rice and stir to make sure that the grains are separate. Add the remaining salt, the remaining spring onions and the prawn mixture. Toss over the heat to mix. Serve hot or cold.

ingredients

50g/2oz cooked **ham**

50g/2oz cooked **prawns,** peeled

3 **eggs**

5ml/1 tsp **salt**

2 **spring onions,** finely chopped

60ml/4 tbsp **vegetable oil**

115g/4oz/1 cup **green peas,**
   thawed if frozen

15ml/1 tbsp **light soy sauce**

15ml/1 tbsp **Chinese rice wine**
   or **dry sherry**

450g/1lb/4 cups cooked **white**
   long grain rice

variation

This is a versatile recipe and is ideal for using up leftovers. Use cooked chicken or turkey instead of the ham, doubling the quantity if you omit the prawns.

rice with dill & broad beans

THIS IS A **FAVOURITE** RICE DISH IN **IRAN**, WHERE IT IS CALLED **BAGHALI POLO**. THE COMBINATION OF BROAD BEANS, DILL AND **WARM SPICES** WORKS VERY WELL, AND THE SAFFRON RICE ADDS A **SPLASH** OF BRIGHT **COLOUR**.

method

SERVES 4

1 Drain the rice, tip it into a saucepan and pour in the water. Add a little salt. Bring to the boil, then lower the heat and simmer very gently for 5 minutes. Drain, rinse well in warm water and drain once again.

2 Melt the butter in a non-stick saucepan. Pour two-thirds of the melted butter into a small jug and set aside. Spoon enough rice into the pan to cover the bottom. Add a quarter of the beans and a little dill. Spread over another layer of rice, then a layer of beans and dill. Repeat the layers until all the beans and dill have been used up, ending with a layer of rice. Cook over a gentle heat for 8 minutes until nearly tender.

3 Pour the reserved melted butter over the rice. Sprinkle with the ground cinnamon and cumin. Cover the pan with a clean dish towel and a tight-fitting lid, lifting the corners of the cloth back over the lid. Cook over a low heat for 25–30 minutes.

4 Spoon about 45ml/3 tbsp of the cooked rice into the bowl of saffron water; mix well. Mound the remaining rice mixture on a large serving plate and spoon the saffron rice on one side to decorate. Serve at once, decorated with the sprig of dill.

ingredients

275g/10oz/1½ cups **basmati rice**, soaked

750ml/1¼ pints/3 cups **water**

40g/1½oz/3 tbsp melted **butter**

175g/6oz/1½ cups frozen **baby broad beans**, thawed and peeled

90ml/6 tbsp finely chopped fresh **dill**, plus 1 fresh **dill sprig**, to garnish

5ml/1 tsp ground **cinnamon**

5ml/1 tsp ground **cumin**

2–3 **saffron strands**, soaked in 15ml/1 tbsp boiling **water**

salt

SERVE THIS **TASTY** DISH WITH BAKED **CHICKEN** OR **FISH**. ADD THE **VEGETABLES** NEAR THE END OF COOKING SO THAT THEY REMAIN **CRISP**.

ingredients

350g/12oz/1¾ cups **basmati rice**
45ml/3 tbsp **vegetable oil**
1 **onion**, chopped
2 **garlic** cloves, crushed
750ml/1¼ pints/3 cups **vegetable stock** or **water**
115g/4oz/⅔ cup fresh or drained canned **sweetcorn kernels**
½ **red** or **green pepper**, seeded and chopped
1 large **carrot**, grated
fresh **chervil** sprigs, to garnish

tanzanian vegetable rice

method   SERVES 4

1 Rinse the rice in a sieve under cold water, then leave to drain thoroughly for about 15 minutes.

2 Heat the oil in a large saucepan and fry the onion for a few minutes over a medium heat until it starts to soften.

3 Add the rice and fry for about 10 minutes, stirring constantly to prevent the rice sticking to the pan. Then stir in the crushed garlic.

4 Pour in the stock or water and stir well. Bring to the boil, then lower the heat, cover and simmer for 10 minutes.

5 Scatter the sweetcorn kernels over the rice, then spread the chopped pepper on top. Sprinkle over the grated carrot. Cover the saucepan tightly. Steam over a low heat until the rice is tender, then mix together with a fork, pile on to a platter and garnish with chervil. Serve immediately.

desserts

USING **SKIMMED MILK** TO MAKE THIS PUDDING IS A **HEALTHY** OPTION, BUT YOU COULD USE **WHOLE MILK** IF YOU PREFER A RICHER, **CREAMIER** TASTE.

ingredients

65g/2½oz/⅓ cup **short grain pudding rice**

45ml/3 tbsp clear **honey**

750ml/1¼ pints/3 cups **skimmed milk**

1 **vanilla pod** or 2.5ml/ ½ tsp **vanilla essence**

butter, for greasing

2 **egg whites**

5ml/1 tsp freshly grated **nutmeg**

wafer biscuits, to serve (optional)

souffléed rice pudding

method   SERVES 4

1 Place the rice, honey and milk in a heavy or non-stick saucepan, and bring the milk to just below boiling point, watching it closely to prevent it from boiling over. Add the vanilla pod, if using.

2 Reduce the heat to the lowest setting and cover the pan. Leave to cook for about 1–1¼ hours, stirring occasionally to prevent sticking, until most of the liquid has been absorbed.

3 Remove the vanilla pod or, if using vanilla essence, add this to the rice mixture now. Preheat the oven to 220°C/425°F/Gas 7. Grease a 1 litre/1¾ pint/4 cup baking dish with butter. and cook for 15–20 minutes until heated through.

4 Place the egg whites in a large grease-free bowl and whisk them until they hold soft peaks. Using either a large metal spoon or a spatula, carefully fold the egg whites evenly into the rice and milk mixture. Tip into the baking dish.

5 Sprinkle with grated nutmeg and bake in the oven for about 15–20 minutes, until the rice pudding has risen well and the surface is golden brown. Serve the pudding hot, with wafer biscuits, if you like.

---
cook's tip

This pudding is delicious topped with a stewed, dried fruit salad.
---

portugese rice pudding

THIS IS **POPULAR** ALL OVER **PORTUGAL** AND IF YOU VISIT THAT COUNTRY YOU'RE LIKELY TO FIND IT ON MOST MENUS. TRADITIONALLY IT IS SERVED **COLD**, BUT IS ACTUALLY DELICIOUS **WARM** AS WELL.

method

SERVES 4

1 Cook the rice in plenty of lightly salted water for about 5 minutes, by which time it will have lost its brittleness.

2 Drain well, then return to the clean pan. Add the milk, lemon rind and butter. Bring to the boil over a moderately low heat, then cover, reduce the heat to the lowest setting and simmer for about 20 minutes or until the rice is thick and creamy.

3 Remove the pan from the heat and allow the rice to cool a little. Remove and discard the lemon rind, then stir in the sugar and the egg yolks. Mix well.

4 Divide among four to six serving bowls and dust with ground cinnamon. Serve cool, with lemon wedges for squeezing.

ingredients

175g/6oz/scant 1 cup **short grain pudding rice**
600ml/1 pint/2½ cups **creamy milk**
2 or 3 strips pared **lemon rind**
65g/2½oz/5 tbsp **butter**, in pieces
115g/4oz/½ cup **caster sugar**
4 **egg** yolks
ground **cinnamon**, for dusting
salt
lemon wedges, to serve

IF YOU'VE NEVER TASTED A **SWEET RISOTTO**, THERE'S A TREAT IN STORE. **CHOCOLATE** RISOTTO IS **DELECTABLE**, AND CHILDREN OF ALL AGES **LOVE IT**.

ingredients

175g/6oz/scant 1 cup **risotto rice**

600ml/1 pint/2½ cups **creamy milk**

75g/3oz **plain chocolate**, broken into pieces

25g/1oz/2 tbsp **butter**

about 50g/2oz/¼ cup **caster sugar**

pinch of ground **cinnamon**

60ml/4 tbsp **double cream**

fresh **raspberries** and **chocolate caraque**, to decorate

chocolate sauce, to serve

chocolate risotto

method

SERVES 4–6

1 Put the rice in a non-stick pan. Pour in the milk and bring to the boil over a low to medium heat. Reduce the heat to the lowest setting and simmer very gently for about 20 minutes, stirring occasionally, until the rice is very soft.

2 Stir in the chocolate, butter and sugar. Cook, stirring all the time over a very gentle heat for 1–2 minutes, until the chocolate has melted.

3 Remove the pan from the heat and stir in the ground cinnamon and double cream. Cover the pan and leave to stand for a few minutes.

4 Spoon the risotto into individual dishes or dessert plates, and decorate with fresh raspberries and chocolate caraque. Serve with chocolate sauce.

caramel rice pudding

THIS **RICE PUDDING** IS DELICIOUS SERVED WITH CRUNCHY **FRESH FRUIT**.

method

SERVES 4–6

1 Preheat the oven to 150°C/300°F/Gas 2. Grease a soufflé dish lightly with a little of the butter. Put the rice in a sieve and wash it thoroughly under cold water. Drain well and put into the soufflé dish.

2 Add 30ml/2 tbsp of the sugar to the dish, with a pinch of salt. Pour on the diluted evaporated milk and stir gently.

3 Dot the surface of the rice with butter. Bake for 2 hours, then leave to cool for 30 minutes.

4 Meanwhile, quarter the pineapple and the figs. Cut the apple into segments and toss in the lemon juice. Preheat the grill.

5 Sprinkle the remaining sugar evenly over the rice. Grill for 5 minutes or until the sugar has caramelized. Leave the rice to stand for 5 minutes to allow the caramel to harden, then serve with the fresh fruit.

ingredients

15g/½oz/1 tbsp **butter**
50g/2oz/¼ cup **short grain pudding rice**
75ml/5 tbsp **demerara sugar**
400g/14oz can **evaporated milk** made up to 600ml/1 pint/ 2½ cups with **water**
2 fresh **baby pineapples**
2 **figs**
1 crisp eating **apple**
10ml/2 tsp **lemon juice**
salt

COOKING **RICE PUDDING** ON TOP OF THE HOB INSTEAD OF IN THE OVEN GIVES IT A LIGHT, **CREAMY** TEXTURE, ESPECIALLY IF YOU REMEMBER TO **STIR** IT FREQUENTLY. IT IS PARTICULARLY **GOOD** SERVED COLD WITH A **TOPPING** OF **FRUIT**, TOASTED **NUTS** OR A TRICKLE OF **HOT CHOCOLATE** SAUCE.

ingredients

50g/2oz/generous ¼ cup **short grain pudding rice**
5ml/1 tsp **vanilla essence**
2.5ml/½ tsp ground **cinnamon**
45ml/3 tbsp **granulated sugar**
600ml/1 pint/2½ cups **milk**

For the toppings
soft berry fruits such as strawberries, raspberries and cherries

variation
For a special occasion, use single cream instead of milk, and glaze the fruit with a little melted redcurrant jelly. (Add a splash of port if you like.)

rice conde sundae

method

SERVES 4

1 Mix the rice, vanilla essence, cinnamon and sugar in a saucepan. Pour in the milk. Bring to the boil, stirring constantly, then reduce the heat so that the mixture barely simmers.

2 Cook the rice over a low heat for 30–40 minutes, stirring frequently. Add extra milk to the rice if it begins to dry out.

3 When the grains are soft, remove the pan from the heat. Allow the rice to cool, stirring it occasionally, then chill.

4 Before serving, stir the rice pudding and spoon it into four sundae dishes. Top with fresh fruits, such as strawberries, raspberries and cherries.

fruited rice ring

THIS **UNUSUAL** RICE PUDDING LOOKS **BEAUTIFUL** TURNED OUT OF A **RING MOULD**, BUT IF YOU PREFER, YOU CAN STIR THE **FRUIT** INTO THE **RICE** AND SERVE IT IN **INDIVIDUAL** DISHES.

method

SERVES 4

1 Mix the rice and milk in a saucepan. Add the cinnamon stick and bring to the boil. Lower the heat, cover the saucepan and simmer, stirring occasionally, for about 1½ hours, until all the liquid has been absorbed.

2 Meanwhile, put the dried fruit salad in a separate pan, pour over the orange juice and bring to the boil. Lower the heat, cover and simmer very gently for about 1 hour, until the fruit is tender and no liquid remains.

3 Remove the cinnamon stick from the rice and gently stir in the caster sugar and grated orange rind.

4 Lightly oil a 1.5 litre/2½ pint/6¼ cup ring tin. Spoon in the fruit so that it covers the bottom of the tin evenly. Top with the rice, smooth it down firmly, then chill until firm.

5 Run a knife around the edge of the ring tin, then invert a serving plate on top. Turn tin and plate over together, then lift off the tin. Serve in slices.

ingredients

65g/2½oz/⅓ cup **short grain pudding rice**
900ml/1½ pints/3¾ cups **semi-skimmed milk**
5cm/2in **cinnamon** stick
175g/6oz/1½ cups **dried fruit salad**
175ml/6fl oz/¾ cup **orange juice**
45ml/3 tbsp **caster sugar**
finely grated rind of 1 small **orange**
sunflower oil, for greasing

ALTHOUGH IT'S **ENTIRELY** POSSIBLE TO COOK THIS BY THE **CONVENTIONAL RISOTTO** METHOD – BY ADDING THE LIQUID SLOWLY – IT MAKES MORE SENSE TO COOK THE RICE WITH THE **MILK**, IN THE SAME WAY AS FOR A **RICE PUDDING**.

ingredients

1 **cooking apple**

15g/1/2oz/1 tbsp **butter**

175g/6oz/scant 1 cup **risotto rice**

600ml/1 pint/2½ cups creamy **milk**

about 50g/2oz/1/4 cup **caster sugar**

1.5ml/1/4 tsp ground **cinnamon**

30ml/2 tbsp **lemon** juice

45ml/3 tbsp **double cream**

grated rind of 1 **lemon**, to decorate

For the poached plums

50g/2oz/1/4 cup light brown **muscovado sugar**

200ml/7fl oz/scant 1 cup **apple juice**

3 **star anise**

cinnamon stick

6 **plums**, halved and sliced

apple & lemon risotto with poached plums

method
SERVES 4

1 Peel and core the apple. Cut it into large chunks. Put these in a large, non-stick pan and add the butter. Heat gently until the butter melts.

2 Add the rice and milk and stir well. Bring to the boil over a medium heat, then simmer very gently for 20–25 minutes, stirring occasionally.

3 To make the poached plums, dissolve the sugar in the apple juice in a pan. Add the spices and bring to the boil. Boil for 2 minutes. Add the plums, and simmer for 2 minutes. Set aside until ready to serve.

4 Stir the sugar, cinnamon and lemon juice into the risotto. Cook for 2 minutes, stirring all the time, then stir in the cream. Taste and add more sugar if necessary. Decorate with the lemon rind and serve with the poached plums.

---

cook's tip
If the apple is very sharp (acidic) the milk may curdle. There is no need to worry about this – it won't affect the look or taste of the sauce.

---

caribbean spiced rice pudding

CARIBBEAN RECIPES CAN BE **EXTREMELY SWEET**, AND YOU MAY FIND YOU CAN REDUCE THE SUGAR IN THIS PUDDING BECAUSE OF THE **NATURAL SWEETNESS** OF THE **FRUIT**.

method

SERVES 4

1 Melt the butter in a non-stick pan and then add the cinnamon stick and sugar. Heat over a medium heat until the sugar begins to caramelize: remove from the heat as soon as this happens.

2 Carefully stir in the rice and three-quarters of the milk. Bring to the boil, stirring all the time, without letting the milk burn. Reduce the heat and simmer for 10 minutes until the rice is cooked, stirring constantly.

3 Add the remaining milk, the allspice and the sultanas. Leave to simmer for 5 minutes, stirring occasionally.

4 When the rice is thick and creamy, allow to cool slightly, then stir in the mandarin and pineapple pieces. As an alternative, the fruit can be served separately, with warm or cold rice.

ingredients

25g/1oz/2 tbsp **butter**

1 **cinnamon** stick

115g/4oz/½ cup soft **brown sugar**

115g/4oz/⅔ cup **ground rice**

1.2 litres/2 pints/5 cups **milk**

2.5ml/½ tsp **allspice**

50g/2oz/⅓ cup **sultanas**

75g/3oz chopped **mandarin oranges**

75g/3oz chopped **pineapple**

index